P9-DFG-701

"Sally Susman knows a great deal about the importance of clear communication to living an authentic life. Her deeply touching and often humorous stories will stay with you and help you navigate and advance in your own professional life."

—**INDRA NOOYI,** former CEO and Chairperson, PepsiCo;
New York Times bestselling author, *My Life in Full*

"*Breaking Through* is a beautifully written, essential work on the importance of communication, full of humor and heart. This book will make you think deeply about expression and how we convey our thoughts, intentions, and needs. Sally Susman delivers a commanding master class and a must-read."

—**MIKA BRZEZINSKI,** cohost of MSNBC's *Morning Joe*,
founder, Know Your Value

"If you want to improve at communication, look no further than those who do it for a living. Sally Susman has devoted her career to bringing clarity to complexity, change, and crisis, and in this book she shares memorable stories and practical insights to help you get heard."

—**ADAM GRANT,** #1 *New York Times* bestselling author,
Think Again; host, TED podcast *ReThinking*

"A brave trailblazer in her field, Sally Susman has helped hundreds of careers flourish—and this book will ensure the success of hundreds of thousands more."

—**RESHMA SAUJANI,** founder, Girls Who Code and Marshall
Plan for Moms

"People like Sally Susman have always known that communication isn't a soft skill—it's the bedrock of business and an absolute requirement for success. Putting her principles to work will help you clarify and reach your goals and be a better leader."

—**ARIANNA HUFFINGTON,** founder and CEO, Thrive Global

"*Breaking Through* is the world's best handbook for how to build and maintain trust at work—and why it's essential for any communications you do. No one could write this book but Sally Susman. Her lessons on how to hear and be heard, how to build and refine your voice, and how to make tough decisions and own them are just as applicable if you're starting your first job or stepping into a new, massive one."

—**DANIEL ROTH,** Editor in Chief and Vice President, LinkedIn

BREAKING THROUGH

BREAKING THROUGH

*Communicating to
Open Minds, Move Hearts,
and Change the World*

SALLY SUSMAN

Chief Corporate Affairs Officer, Pfizer

Harvard Business Review Press

Boston, Massachusetts

HBR Press Quantity Sales Discounts

Harvard Business Review Press titles are available at significant quantity discounts when purchased in bulk for client gifts, sales promotions, and premiums. Special editions, including books with corporate logos, customized covers, and letters from the company or CEO printed in the front matter, as well as excerpts of existing books, can also be created in large quantities for special needs.

For details and discount information for both print and ebook formats, contact booksales@harvardbusiness.org, tel. 800-988-0886, or www.hbr.org/bulksales.

Copyright 2023 Sally Susman

All rights reserved

Printed in the United States of America

10 9 8 7 6 5 4 3 2 1

No part of this publication may be reproduced, stored in or introduced into a retrieval system, or transmitted, in any form, or by any means (electronic, mechanical, photocopying, recording, or otherwise), without the prior permission of the publisher. Requests for permission should be directed to permissions@harvardbusiness.org, or mailed to Permissions, Harvard Business School Publishing, 60 Harvard Way, Boston, Massachusetts 02163.

The web addresses referenced in this book were live and correct at the time of the book's publication but may be subject to change.

Cataloging-in-Publication data is forthcoming.

ISBN: 978-1-64782-395-5
eISBN: 978-1-64782-396-2

The paper used in this publication meets the requirements of the American National Standard for Permanence of Paper for Publications and Documents in Libraries and Archives Z39.48-1992.

For Robin and Lily

For Albert

CONTENTS

Preface: Your Reputation Is Your Most Precious Asset   ix

1   **What Am I Trying to Say?**   1

    Channel Your Intention

2   **Sticking Your Neck Out**   19

    Muster the Courage for Candor

3   **Am I Boring You?**   39

    Stay Curious, Be Creative

4   **Do Manners Matter Anymore?**   57

    The Strength of Being Gracious and Kind

5   **Measure Up to the Moment**   73

    Take Time to Pause and Prepare

6   **Can You Hear Me Now?**   95

    Perfect Your Pitch

7   **Hey! Who's Going to Get the Credit?**   111

    Disarm with Humility, Empower with Truth

8   **Lighten Up!**   131

Delight with Humor

9   **Look for Answers in the Rearview Mirror**   149

Reflect and Honor

10 **Why Is Everybody So Angry?**   169

Seek Harmony

Notes   189
Index   193
Acknowledgments   201
About the Author   203

Your Reputation Is Your Most Precious Asset

During the cold night of February 24, 2022, Russian President Vladimir Putin deployed an airstrike against Ukraine. The next morning, he launched a ground invasion with armored tanks and troops. These hostilities triggered the largest refugee crisis since World War II as more than 6 million people streamed from Ukraine into neighboring countries. The world watched the atrocities in disbelief. I was horrified.

The invasion was swiftly and widely condemned. The United Nations General Assembly adopted a resolution demanding a full withdrawal. Prominent companies including Starbucks, McDonald's, Disney, and many others withdrew their products from Russia in the weeks that followed. The West was exerting moral, political, and economic pressure to end this war.

At Pfizer, where I'm the chief corporate affairs officer, we had a problem. As providers of essential medicines, biopharmaceutical companies historically have been carved out of economic sanctions on humanitarian grounds. Of course, that made sense. A Russian kid with cancer is like any kid with cancer and deserves treatment. We continued to send our medicines and vaccines without disruption.

Over a weekend in early March, my boss and Pfizer's dynamic chairman and CEO, Albert Bourla, directed us to take a hard look at ourselves and our options. Other chief executives might have chosen not to wade in. They may have felt the status quo would be sufficient and end the discussion there. In years past, when companies believed it best to keep their heads down and avoid politics, that may have been enough. But not now. Senior executives are expected to speak out based on their values, lead with purpose, and use their platforms to steer the global discussion. These proactive ideals can be vague, symbolic gestures if companies fail to take bold and specific actions when necessary.

Albert has a seemingly innate sense of fast-moving public opinion shifts and a great touch at corporate policy-making. He peppered us with all the right questions: Would we appear to be ducking behind the historic precedence that exempted medicine makers? Would we be seen to be conducting business as usual? And most importantly, how could we maintain our medical exemption from the sanctions against Russia, but still make a stronger statement based on our principles?

We were walking a tightrope.

Albert, several of my peers on the leadership team, and I brainstormed what else we could do. We batted ideas back and forth over rapid-fire emails, with the needs of patients always top of mind. We were sensitive to the expectations, inside and outside the company, for moral leadership. That Sunday I refined our messages and circulated drafts that included bolder steps.

On Monday morning, March 14, 2022, Pfizer issued a statement saying that, while we would maintain a humanitarian supply of medicines to Russia, we would also contribute all profits made there to directly support the Ukrainians. Also, we announced that we would not initiate new clinical trials in Russia or make planned investments with local suppliers intended to build manufacturing capacity.

Our statement was sent to all employees and posted on our website. Immediately, I felt proud of my company for finding the narrow, but essential path forward. We preserved our principle of putting the patient first while also making clear that we opposed the Russian aggression. The response from our colleagues and the media to our statement was very positive.

I don't know how the invasion of Ukraine will end, but I do know one thing: Pfizer's Russia statement was the latest, but not the last, example of how communications and leadership are not only entwined, but inseparable.

What a company says is synonymous with what it is and what it believes. Taking carefully considered, courageous positions is the new standard. Whether the issue is geopolitics, rising inequality, or climate change, business leaders are expected to have a view. Employees, consumers, regulators, investors, the media, governance experts, and our children are watching.

Because of this increased scrutiny and the elevated stakes, communications can no longer be considered a soft skill. The ability to lead and drive the public conversation is a rock-hard competency. It tests one's abilities as much as any professional discipline, maybe more so in a time when public trust in business, government, and media is at an all-time low. Much of what passes as civil discourse has plummeted into useless and degrading attacks. Families fight over politics at the holiday dinner table. Neighbor is pitted against neighbor over social issues. We're living in a depersonalized digital world where faceless opponents can anonymously smear, influence, stalk, and ghost us.

The erosion of civility is heartbreaking to witness, but not irreversible. I'm convinced that with the right mindset, we can build communications muscles that help us maintain and expand the traditions of storytelling, narration, dialogue, and constructive debate. Common ground and shared ambitions are still possible. As a society and as individuals, we can cut through the noise and clutter to open minds, move hearts, and shift the dialogue in a positive direction. In fact, we must, and that's why I am writing this book.

How I Got Here

The seeds of my personal mission of civility, constructive engagement, and leadership were planted by my parents. My folks were strict, especially when it came to having good manners. From a young age, I was taught to introduce myself by making eye contact, using a clear voice, and offering a firm handshake.

As a girl, I wanted to be either an investigative journalist or the mayor of my hometown, St. Louis, Missouri. While neither of those noble professions panned out, I'm fortunate to have found a career in corporate affairs that lets me live out those early interests. My days are full of crafting narratives, analyzing politics, and advocating for policies. Now I'm sixty and have become a cheerleader for my profession.

I assure you my success was far from guaranteed. My teachers would have voted me *least* likely to succeed. I struggled, made missteps, and misread signposts along the way. In hindsight, these were rookie mistakes many of us make. Let's face it, we all stumble in professional potholes. I hope this book bolsters your resiliency, allowing you to brush off the inevitable scrapes and bruises with the salve of advice, wisdom, and solutions offered on these pages.

I share both triumphant and humiliating moments in this book. Some anecdotes are from growing up in an ambitious family, and many of the principles in this book were formed and are based on what I learned from my parents. When I left for college, my father handed me an envelope with a heartfelt letter written on yellow legal pad paper. It said, "Your reputation is your most precious asset." Dad was right about that.

My father was a mentor and role model. Originally a lawyer, he became the primary volunteer fundraiser for Thomas Eagleton, who was running for US Senate in 1968. Eagleton's victory turned my dad into a kingmaker and our household into a hub for political candidates and elected officials seeking support. My brother, Billy, and I were schlepped to big Democratic conferences and national conventions. My parents coached us to listen respectfully and speak up when spoken to, habits that continue to serve me today. I'm grateful for my parents' training to be a strong, respectful, and diplomatic communicator.

My parents' shared vision and hard work paid off when, in 2009, President Barack Obama appointed my father to be the US Ambassador to the Court of St. James in the United Kingdom. From this most prestigious post, my parents wrote the final chapters of their professional and personal stories. It's against this backdrop of dreams fueled by discipline and opportunities born of hard work that I forged my own passions and believed that those things I loved, writing and politics, would lead to a fulfilling livelihood.

I followed their footsteps in both Washington and, later, corporate adventures. I volunteered on many presidential and statewide campaigns (most crashing in defeat) and began my career working first in the US Senate and then as a political appointee in the Clinton administration. Politics was a crucial proving ground as I learned how to communicate with angry constituents, support leaders under pressure, and build coalitions. These stories figure into this book and underpin the principles I espouse.

Ultimately, I made my career in business and believe in the power of the private sector as a force for good. Learning at the side of some of business's brightest lights, I moved up the ranks in communications departments, first at the American Express Company, known for its visually stunning and groundbreaking marketing communications.

Later, I joined The Estée Lauder Companies where I had the honor of working closely with the Lauder family. Estée Lauder, a master communicator, claims to have built her empire on the communications theory, "Telephone, Telegraph, Tell a Woman." She understood what it meant to go viral long before the phrase was in the public lexicon.

I spent seven years as the executive vice president and chief communications officer for The Estée Lauder Companies. Many of my principles are drawn from my experiences working with this iconic company and extraordinary family.

By the time I left Estée Lauder, I was itching for something bigger and more meaningful. This is not to say that my work at Lauder was unimportant or that the business of the company was trivial. Rather, I felt I had learned all I could there and wanted to do something harder.

In 2007, I joined Pfizer and seriously overshot that mark of doing something more difficult. I was naive about what an uphill battle I would face as the company's chief communications officer. In my early days at Pfizer, I almost quit on multiple occasions for fear I couldn't take the hostility the company faced. Still, I hung in there and remained devoted to the idea of turning around the negative impression of Big Pharma and reversing the cynicism that pervades the general view of these companies that make lifesaving medicines and vaccines. It was the ultimate communications challenge, and I was game.

My close friends tried to intervene and begged me at the time *not* to work for Big Pharma. It had a horrendous reputation, not very far behind tobacco companies in the public's mind. There was good reason for the skepticism. Some in the industry *had* broken the public trust. Pharma had such a powerful stigma that, after I took the job, I became the lady no one wanted to talk to at cocktail parties or sit next to on long plane rides. It was more painful than I had anticipated.

For more than a decade I put my shoulder to the wheel representing Pfizer, its leaders, scientists, and lifesaving medicines and vaccines. I came to enjoy working at the center of health-care policy and big business on a global stage. During those years, I liked to believe I was making steady, if slow, progress to build the company's profile, always mindful of the adage that "reputation is earned in drops and lost in buckets."

Then the Covid-19 pandemic hit. Everything was upended. Professionally, I felt caught in a riptide. My company was promising to deliver a vaccine in record time. The world was depending on us. But there was also a strong undercurrent of fear and anxiety. Vaccine skepticism, suspicion around Big Pharma's motives, apprehension about the US government's shifting recommendations of so-called lockdowns, economic insecurity, political polarization, civil unrest, and just plain fear were challenges we had to recognize and respect. But we also had to address those challenges in a way that didn't alienate people but, instead, brought them into the conversation. Was I up to the task? I didn't have a choice. I'd have to be.

This Book Is for You

For most of my career I believed I needed to be "in the room where it happened." When I became a boss, I proselytized that view to my team, urging them to earn a seat at the company table. I'm sure they considered me the grouch-in-chief as I railed against summer Fridays, the corporate fad where employees could knock off early for weekends during the summer months. Equally, I was not a believer in the work-from-home movement. As communications counselors, I thought my team and I needed to be on the scene, sleeves rolled up.

During the eighteen months that many Pfizer colleagues worked remotely during the pandemic, we did an astonishing amount of business, and did it well. In some cases, such as our need to connect with business and government leaders around the world, it was more efficient to Zoom rather than travel the traditional way. The pandemic had proved me wrong . . . mostly.

One activity was still missing and could not be replaced. That was the crucial apprenticeship of the new and younger members of my profession. Unlike my colleagues who are scientists and statisticians, lawyers and regulators, where specific professional degrees and licensing are required, communications work is mainly learned by an apprentice period that can take years, even decades in some cases

(I'm still learning). Training by toiling under an expert reminds me of the work of blacksmiths around a firepit or young cooks watching a head chef. Some things just must be observed over time. How do I know this? Because it is how I learned.

In 1990, I joined American Express and was fortunate to get a position (at the very bottom) in its public relations department. On my visits to the executive floor, I saw Joan Spero, a woman at the top of the corporate affairs function to which the PR team reported (a breakthrough in and of itself in those days). I watched how she spoke and carried herself. I saw the kind of global projects she engaged in and when she thought it wiser to take a pass. I watched her every move. The same is true of subsequent bosses I had in my field. From each I took away tidbits of knowledge, nuts I squirreled away for the seasons that were to come.

Now that I'm leading the team, teaching moments are my greatest pleasure. During remote working, I missed the chances to huddle with colleagues around the table to bang out a solution; the moments when someone comes in, closes the door, and asks a question that's been plaguing them; the times when we just hung out and swapped stories over a greasy pizza.

Even in those seemingly casual moments, I try to equip those around me with the tools to feel heard and understood and to break through in whatever realm they choose. That is my hope for you, too.

Breaking Through lays out the ten leadership and communications tenets that I have refined and practiced over decades working in the field. I have recently come to fully appreciate their effectiveness, as clarified for me by the pandemic's crucible. These essential tenets for effective, respectful engagement are also values that have helped me see things anew and allowed me to successfully encourage others to thoughtfully consider uncomfortable ideas and challenging views. They have assisted me in delighting and inspiring others in stressful situations as well as times of relative calm. Intentionality, candor, preparation, and reflection, among others, open the door for understanding and a willingness to embrace new ways of thinking.

The ideas in *Breaking Through* offer something different, accessible, progressive, and respectful. I know my strategies work because I've used them for more than three (OK, closer to four) decades during difficult personal and professional moments, culminating with the historically unprecedented two years when I, in my role at Pfizer, was tasked with leading what has been called one of the most urgent, high-stakes public dialogues of the last century. Not only did they help me survive while we rolled out the novel vaccine, building confidence in a new lifesaving technology and helping make complex science accessible to the global community, these strategies also helped me thrive with a renewed sense of purpose in all of my communications, personal and professional. They can do the same for you.

The principles in this book are universal. They have been honed through study, trial, and error, and from observing people who've influenced and inspired me, some of whom you will hear from in this book, such as the former American Express chairman and chief executive officer, Ken Chenault; the first Republican female White House press secretary, Dana Perino; and a world-class restaurateur and hospitality guru, Danny Meyer. While my path to developing these principles was unique, I am convinced they are essential for all of us who strive to:

- Make all kinds of conversations more empathetic, dynamic, and productive

- Introduce bold new ideas or transformational products

- Persuade others to join a movement or back a cause

- Reverse course when caught in the glare of negative public opinion

These lessons are not for chief executives and press secretaries only. They are for professionals of any stripe or level. They are for students, too. I've lectured in colleges and universities, sharing these ideas with English majors and candidates for a master's in business administration. Superlative communications skills will serve you well regardless of your career trajectory.

I try to tell these stories honestly and with as much humor and humility as I can, *always* mindful of readers' expectations to gain insight into new, surprising, and ultimately highly applicable ways for their own communications challenges and aspirations. You can read the book in a linear fashion or cherry-pick the principles that speak most directly to you. You can read some chapters, set this book aside, and then pick it up again when you need it most. If all else fails, you can use it as a doorstop.

I didn't think there would be a pandemic when I took the Pfizer job. Who really believes something like that will happen in their lifetime? When it hit, I had to use every muscle I had, and some I didn't know I had, to communicate Pfizer's role in solving a global challenge. I believe I was built for that moment.

The principles I share in *Breaking Through* not only helped me navigate, but proved to be essential in making a complex public health crisis understandable to a wide array of people, including how we could come through it safely for the public and stronger as a company, too.

As the world now knows, the Pfizer/BioNTech Covid-19 vaccine was found to be incredibly effective, and our plans to manufacture it safely and at scale were highly successful. So, too, our communications strategy was a success, evidenced by the number of people who felt comfortable and even eager to be vaccinated, and a dramatically transformed view of Pfizer. This was a key part of the overall success, and I'll dig into the details of how we made it work.

You never know when life-altering and world-changing moments like a pandemic will come, but those who know history, or who have lived through devastations like wars, terrorist attacks, destructive weather, or stock market crashes, know crises will occur. We just don't know when. You may find yourself in the middle of such events—on the front lines, at the microphone, dispensing information, being relied on. Best be ready.

I'd like nothing more than to help you prepare. The fascinating, relevant work of communications is learned best by apprenticeship, watching others with greater real-world experience. That's how I learned. I owe thanks to many bosses who taught me by their example. By sharing my principles through this book, I wish to replicate that opportunity for you.

That's why I spent my early mornings and weekends writing this book. I am devoted to helping you—whether communications is your profession, your passion, or just a tool to help you get through the day. In the end, I believe you want to make a difference, feel heard, and be understood so you can break through to a wider audience with a deeper connection. I hope this book will become your trusted field guide, primer, and friend in these pursuits. Here we go.

BREAKING THROUGH

CHAPTER ONE

What Am I Trying to Say?

Channel Your Intention

I AM NOT A YOGI, BUT I DO ENJOY AN OCCASIONAL YOGA class, if only to be in sweaty proximity to the lithe and enlightened. I'm the one in baggy shorts and an old T-shirt who has placed her mat at the back of the class, praying that the teacher will call "shavasana" so I can drop into the supine position.

Even though I'm an infrequent (and inflexible) practitioner, I was saddened when, in late February 2020, my local yoga studio closed due to Covid fears. On Sunday, March 1, I was alone on my living room floor, cross-legged on my mat, streaming a yoga session on my smartphone. Instead of meditating on the great nothingness that yogis like to extol, I was more engaged with the real world than I should have been. My house was quiet, but my head was noisy. I was unable to slow and deepen my breathing. Worries kept scrolling in my mind. I couldn't gentle down or settle in.

I had been unnerved by a call I placed early that morning. "It's eerie. The streets of Beijing are empty," Pfizer's senior leader in our China division reported when we talked during the dawn hours. He and I rarely spoke, but I had reached out to him in my role as chief corporate affairs officer at Pfizer, and also as a fellow human; I was troubled over his well-being. I had been paying careful attention to news reports coming out of Wuhan concerning a virus that was moving quickly through the city's population. He confirmed that health officials in China were issuing warnings about a mysterious virus that laid low otherwise healthy people with an undiagnosed flu-like sickness; some became so ill they were unable to breathe without a ventilator.

"I'm so grateful you called to check on me," he continued. I heard desperation in the voice of a man I knew to be steady and stoic. The virus had been recently identified as something I'd never heard of: SARS-CoV-2. It was a new or "novel" form of the coronavirus that has been around for centuries. It had just begun to demonstrate to scientists and researchers its significant ability to spread quickly from person to person.

At the time, prominent doctors and infectious disease researchers believed this highly contagious virus most likely spread by droplets through the air. The media reported cases were spiraling across the globe. I joined millions of people who watched in shock and disbelief as news reports recorded the global, national, and local caseloads. The death toll ticked up hourly. Ten days later, the World Health Organization would declare Covid-19 a global pandemic.

I also recalled disturbing emotions from the night before, when I felt my own panic rising as I walked home after having dinner with a friend in Greenwich Village. My wife was out of town, visiting family on a ski trip. She's immunocompromised, and I was concerned about her. I called her from my cell phone as I walked across 14th Street under a quiet that was unusual even for a frigid evening in Manhattan.

"Something's not right here," I said. "Hurry home."

I imagined millions of others making similar calls to loved ones.

"You worry too much," she replied. It's true, I do. But this felt different.

Something was in the air aside from the chill, and I could feel it. I saw it when I stopped in at my corner bodega. The shelves were thinned out. A couple of rolls of paper towels sat on a metal shelf, their wrapping askew. No toilet paper at all. Bread and milk, the survival talismans of any crisis, were severely depleted. A hoarder's instinct I never knew I had was triggered. The friendly counterman looked like a deer caught in the headlights—we gazed at each other with a mutual feeling of unease, he and I united in fear for a moment. I thought about buying cigarettes, though I had quit more than twenty-five years ago. How could there be no hand soap or paper towels in New York City? I felt the fight-or-flight impulse kick in. But where would I go?

Home. I had to get home. But, with my wife away and my young adult daughter locked down in a hot zone in California, my house would be dark. I left the store empty-handed and scared.

Mostly, I was contemplating the brave mission my company was pursuing in developing a vaccine at lightning speed. Fortunately, my extraordinary boss, Pfizer's chairman and CEO Albert Bourla, had just made a powerful pledge. From the start he knew exactly what he intended: to find a vaccine before the fall when this deadly virus would likely double back in a devastating second wave with the cold weather. "We will make the impossible, possible," Albert said. I believed we would find the vaccine. I had to. The alternative was unthinkable.

This mission to find the vaccine presented me with a rare opportunity to be part of a moonshot that could potentially save millions of lives. For me it had the added possibility to repair the abysmal reputation of Big Pharma. This was urgent, not only for business reasons but because it was essential that we earn the trust of many skeptical people if we were to be recognized as legitimate contributors to the war against a virus that was not yet well understood in terms of spread and mortality. Imagine the compounded tragedy if we developed a safe and effective vaccine that no one had the confidence to take. We had to build back much of the trust the industry had lost . . . and fast. This was a communications challenge I had prepared for my entire career. It wasn't only the vaccine science that would be groundbreaking, but the intense engagement with the public as well. So very much was on the line.

The Moment Arrives

The Covid-19 crisis had forced people to rethink many things: Where and how should they live? How would they educate their kids? Who would they trust to be in their pod? Maybe this virus could also upend their long-entrenched hostility toward the biopharmaceutical industry. Perhaps the industry that everyone—Democrats and Republicans, the elderly and the young, the wealthy and the needy—loved to hate might be the savior in what became a terrifying pandemic.

I had no doubt that this would be a trying time morally, professionally, and even spiritually. Maybe the yoga could help with the latter, but in the coming days I would need to find the right words to convey what Pfizer was doing to beat this once-in-a-century plague.

This moment, with so much suffering and death, did not lend itself to the tried-and-true crisis communications exercises. I couldn't rely on the basic playbook that every communications graduate student and entry-level professional has been taught—the campaign plan that begins with an ambitious goal, a smart strategy of reliable and non-controversial techniques along with an accompanying set of detailed supporting tactics and maneuvers. Sure, the conventional methods that I've employed over my career worked in other industries or even for other scientific breakthroughs, but not now. No way. This Covid crisis and the velocity with which it was undermining public confidence and was susceptible to rumor would require something more.

Consumers are also savvy; they are already wary of pharmaceutical company communications. Too many advertisements showing happy people running through grass fields while a voiceover gives a long list of potential side effects had eroded our credibility. People wouldn't accept a hackneyed approach when it came to injecting a new vaccine into their bodies and those of their loved ones. At least not without asking a lot of complex and valid questions.

We needed something more powerful and less predictable if we were to succeed in creating confidence and trust in our work at a time of such justifiably profound anxiety. My communications, government relations, patient advocacy, and public affairs planning needed ambitions of equal magnitude to those our company was setting: a first-time vaccine technology shot into arms within a year to save the world. Nothing less would do, but there were few if any lessons from the past that we could draw on.

Still on my mat, I recalled my favorite point in any yoga class. At the start of a session, the teacher suggests we set an intention for our yoga practice. It's a quiet, reflective time just before I hoist my creaky self into downward-facing dog. Blessings for my loved ones or epiphanies to answer my deepest nagging questions float into my mind. Often the sentiment sticks with me all day. Setting an intention focused me on who I wanted to be in the moment, helped me recognize my values, and raised my emotional and physical energy.

That is the moment it came to me.

Between deep ujjayi breaths, the idea of what was required of me in this exceptional time was clear. I needed an intention.

"My intention is to break through," I said, chanting it aloud to myself.

What does that mean? That I wasn't looking to merely modify views in the moment. No, I was striving for a truly new and enduring understanding of what my company could do and what we stood for.

The breakthrough intention became my über-idea, a big overarching thought that would hover above all our work. To cut through the noise and fear, we needed to shatter everything the public believed to be true about Big Pharma (and Pfizer is one of the biggest of the big). We had to challenge every assumption and respond respectfully to every criticism. We had to rethink the very essence of our public profile. We had to reintroduce ourselves.

I didn't have the scientific skills to discover a novel vaccine, but I could craft and roll out its surround-sound narrative. Session over! I rolled up my yoga mat, got off the floor, and opened my computer.

"Listen," I said to my team on a hastily arranged video conference call. "Forget the old rules of how we operate. Imagine we are founders of a startup, not a 171-year-old company. I'm no longer interested in playing defense or dodging the broadsides against our industry. This is our moment to strike out and break through to people. What do you think?"

In their response, I learned my first lesson about the power of a meaningful intention. My team was longing for it. They were eager (maybe desperate) to hitch the wagon of their work to a bolder, brighter star. I felt their energy rise. Why hadn't I done this sooner when we weren't in a crisis? I wish I had.

That morning, we discussed what fulfilling the intention to create breakthrough communications meant: the risks we would have to take; how we would have to be more forthcoming and transparent and make ourselves more available. I encouraged them, and myself, to let go of the defensiveness that had become routine during all these years of public criticism of the drug industry. I urged them to be bolder and enter a new world of possibilities for human connection and communication.

We would not find excuses for what could not be done. Absolutely everyone was on board and fully motivated, ready to commit to the intention. Immediately, from our kitchens and basements, connecting over video calls, we set to work.

I'm fortunate to lead a highly talented and intensely dedicated crew of corporate affairs professionals. Teams like ours were built for scenarios like this: when complex corporate ambitions intersect with deep-felt human emotion. Thankfully, my department encompasses communications including speechwriting, product publicity, social media, and a press office; government relations including state, federal, and major capitals across the globe; a policy shop that acts as an in-house think tank; a corporate responsibility group that directs our foundation and leads our sustainability efforts; a patient advocacy team; and an investor relations group. We had the people with all the skills that we required to meet the intention. Whether you belong to a large team or a small one, whether you're in an agency or are a sole contributor or a job applicant, the power of setting a clear guiding intention is equally valid.

The contemporary corporate affairs group, like the one I lead, is a relatively new function. It was conceived of and fortified to anticipate and respond to urgent needs created by an ever more vocal and demanding set of stakeholders, like environmentalists, patient advocates, human rights leaders, and others who are driven by legitimate and strong passions. These people believe they deserve a say in how companies should operate. They are not wrong. Powerful groups of agitated people can bring a company or a government to its knees. To successfully break through to the public during a pandemic, we couldn't dismiss these groups and their concerns. We mustn't shuffle them off to the side. We would need to enlist them, earn their trust, and get their help.

Examples from the past gave me healthy respect for mission-driven stakeholders. My first memory of powerful intention-led activism was the boycott against the South African apartheid system with a call to stop purchasing products from the country. These actions helped to overturn the morally bankrupt regime. Another example is the AIDS activists who, in the 1980s, pointed their fear and rage at the medical and scientific establishment, ultimately forcing those communities to change the way they conducted research and paving the way for the discovery of treatments that have saved the lives of millions worldwide. More recently, in 2018, a boycott was marshaled against the National Rifle Association for its failure to respond to the torrent of gun violence in American schools. Public pressure also caused several gun retailers to raise the age required to buy firearms and place other restrictions on gun sales. Without question, stakeholder activism is a potent force.

There were times when I ducked the overtures from stakeholders, hoping they wouldn't turn their angry glare on my employers. Perhaps I had a certain level of defensiveness and skepticism from years of tense, unproductive exchanges. These engagements often ended in stalemate—each side leaving the discussion exactly where they started, on opposite sides. I'll never forget the time I heard a group of diabetes patients claim that the pharmaceutical industry had a cure for their disease but kept it secret because a lifetime of insulin was more profitable. That allegation made me cry.

There were times when these caustic exchanges made me want to dig a deep moat around my office and pull up the drawbridge. But, if we were going to achieve breakthroughs while people were physically and emotionally locked down, we needed to get ahead of every argument and be in favor with every interested party. As breakthrough communicators, this was our charge. Open the gates, let down the drawbridges, and dry the moat. Invite them in. Welcome the debate. Listen as well as speak. Never stonewall with silence.

Given the pandemic's scope, there was a broader set of interested constituency groups we'd rarely engaged with before, including teachers unions, retailers, government agencies, and advocacy organizations. Some of the leaders of these groups represented a fresh list of power players; others had been more adversarial in the past. Now, we had to extend a hand of partnership. With our new intention to debunk myths and dismantle historic distrust, we had to turn these potential detractors into advocates.

Launching the Breakthrough Intention

Fueled by this powerful intention, there was no door on which I wouldn't knock. I got creative about our roster of alliances. I reached out to Randi Weingarten, president of the American Federation of

Teachers. A straight talker and a tough negotiator, Weingarten's reputation preceded her. She quizzed me about the timetable for the vaccine and its effectiveness. I shared what we knew, wanting to help her plan for when the nearly 2 million teachers she represented could safely return to the classroom. Millions of students and their parents across the country were counting on those teachers. The stakes were higher than I'd ever imagined.

A few days later, I jumped on a Zoom call with a group of retailers from around the country who had concerns about when their stores and malls might reopen. How could they protect their workforces? When might they be able to purchase vaccines privately for their employees? When did we think the public would feel confident to enter the stores? Again, without pretending to have all the answers, I shared all the relevant information we had. "Thanks for showing up today," the host said when the session was ending.

We talked regularly to governors across the country to share what we knew about the necessary preparations they would need to make to be ready to receive the vaccine if and when it was authorized in the months ahead. Partisan politics did not play a role at all, nor did it have a place in this effort. We didn't care whether the letter D or R was next to the governor's name. We wanted to help everyone in every state. Elected officials with whom we had previously struggled to connect were reaching out to us. We not only took their inbound calls but developed pilot programs and special educational seminars to help them.

With engagements like these, I put our stakeholder strategy on steroids. We no longer waited for the phone to ring, but instead reached out to them, frequently bringing our top scientists and business leaders with us to educate at every turn. Guided by my intention to shatter the status quo, we shifted from defense to offense. We traded in our fears for an exciting sense of new possibilities. We were making progress scientifically, and we were opening minds and moving hearts, even among those most entrenched against us.

Our intention to reintroduce ourselves and communicate in ways that would reestablish trust meant we had to ditch the arrogance and engage in conversations, even if we didn't have all the answers. Mindful of all the appropriate regulations and always in consultation with our legal team, we found a way to get closer to people. We were no longer finding ourselves at arm's length from the public. Covid restrictions may have required social distancing, but we were truly connecting with people. We were listening, and we were being heard. Those relationships proved vital over the months that followed, offering us fellowship along the journey.

Albert Bourla was my breakthrough guru. When Albert became Pfizer's CEO in January 2019, he unveiled a new purpose statement for the company: "Breakthroughs That Change Patients' Lives." Surely, this new rallying cry planted the first seeds in my mind about the power of breakthroughs. For that, and so much more, I'm grateful to Albert. He is my friend, my boss, and a peerless leader. I didn't write "fearless," because undoubtedly Albert had frightful moments in the high-stakes race for a vaccine. I specifically call him "peerless" because thanks to Albert's singular vision and sturdy backbone, Pfizer found a highly effective and safe mRNA vaccine and was the first to manufacture and distribute it on a massive scale.

I've worked with nine chief executive officers and reported directly to six. I've studied what it means to sit in the ultimate corner office, and I've experienced a wide range of styles, from the wealth creators and diplomats to the appeasers and placeholders. I know that nothing is a greater symbol of a company's character than its chief executive.

When the pandemic hit, Albert was a relatively new CEO and still largely unknown. If we were to achieve our breakthrough intention, he'd have to step out into the spotlight and be the voice of the industry. I needed to build his profile quickly and smartly. As our leader, Albert would be the most visible proof point of our intention to put a stake in the ground as a company transforming. He was essential to my breakthrough communications plan.

A Greek Jew, a veterinarian with a heavy accent, Albert is not your typical Big Pharma CEO. Like most leaders, he is driven and demanding. Albert expects a lot from his team, too. But he can also be funny and uses humor in a sensitive way to diffuse awkward situations. Never at arm's length, he is always right there with us, willing to roll up his sleeves when there is a problem to solve or to offer a shoulder if you needed bolstering. Of course, Albert's quest to "make the impossible, possible" led to some tense exchanges for all of us on the team. But, for a company seeking a full image overhaul from the perception that we were arrogant and uncaring, Albert was like a gift from central casting. His open and gregarious manner surprised and charmed people. He was our breakthrough poster boy. We all followed his lead and got personally involved in scaling the walls of skepticism, the hard labor of trust-building, often traveling outside our comfort zones.

Albert pushed us to the brink with seemingly impossible demands and then circled back for quiet conversations to understand our struggles and help us overcome obstacles. He has an ability to both pressure and nurture his team in just the right measure. How does he do that? By making sure he knows us as individuals. He understands who sandbags their goals to overachieve, who sets sky-high targets driven by their own ambition, who requires a kick in the pants, and who needs to be spoken to in supportive tones. Albert's bespoke management of senior leaders was key to our ability to create a Food and Drug Administration–authorized vaccine in eight months versus the usual ten-year time frame.

Suddenly, our previously invisible scientists were like superheroes. We booked them on all the major networks and cable channels. Our chief scientific officer, Mikael Dolsten, was a repeat guest on the *Today Show* via Zoom interviews from his bedroom. Mikael would ultimately shepherd the greatest medical advance in a century, but I still had to remind him to make his bed before clicking on his computer camera for the interview. We were less defensive about granting interviews and more open to unusual formats and audiences. Moving beyond medical journals, our scientific experts were featured in *Forbes*,

Fast Company, and *People* magazine, which exposed our team's work to a general audience.

Scientists are not necessarily natural spokespeople, so we worked differently, and darn effectively, during the pandemic. We kept things fluid and didn't wait for formal discussions to announce milestones or correct misunderstandings. Our dialogue with the science team became more open and ongoing. Regular check-ins allowed us to craft updates more quickly and to swiftly respond to requests and tackle misinformation. We also capitalized on our scientists' rich and varied experiences, allowing their personal interests to shine through. For example, Bill Gruber, Pfizer's lead vaccine developer, is a soft-spoken and humble pediatrician with a passion for making vaccines for children. We drafted Bill for the *NBC Nightly News* Kids Edition and many other interviews where he could soothe anxieties and answer questions from kids, parents, and caregivers. With each success, the team's confidence grew.

Now that our scientists and executive team had jumped into the fray, I had to up my game, too. It wasn't easy for me. It may be surprising, but I'm an introvert. I draw energy from the quiet pursuits of reading and writing. For me, prolonged exposure to people can be draining. I'm most comfortable behind the scenes. I also knew that if I was going to make good on our breakthrough intention, I'd have to step forward. I was nervous. Over the fourteen years I had worked at the company, I'd grown accustomed to, and been occasionally burned by, heat against the pharma industry. It pains me to say that I didn't always rise to the challenge. I once heard a man groan when he learned he was seated next to "the lady from Big Pharma" at a dinner party. I've been attacked at family gatherings for my career path, and I learned from experience to never reveal my profession to my seatmates on airplanes.

Unfortunately, the old saying "She has a face for radio" could have been written for me. Luckily, podcasts have grown in popularity and were particularly well suited for a time when people were stuck at home and looking for information and entertainment. I was invited on many podcasts, including top political strategist Bradley Tusk's *Firewall* for entrepreneurs and disrupters and *Greater*, a podcast focused on leadership in New York City hosted by major Gothamites and civic leaders Cheryl Effron and Jamie Rubin. Later I even volunteered for a few television appearances. Through these interviews I found a workable platform to tell Pfizer's story and, more importantly, I found my voice.

Before the pandemic, I often spoke about subjects on Pfizer's periphery, like promoting our charitable initiatives, or I cut the ribbon at a new community program. I relegated myself to the sidelines, never quite sure I had the goods. At Pfizer, I often found myself the only person in the room without an advanced degree. Now in the race to deliver a vaccine, I was drafted into something bigger than myself, more powerful than my doubts. I spoke out with messages that cut to the core: showcasing the groundbreaking work of my colleagues; connecting the dots between our knowledge and the public's hunger for information; understanding people's fear and building confidence for our vaccine. Outside my own bunker, I felt less like a staffer and more like a principal, both relevant *and* revitalized. The intention was not only helping the company but recharging my own batteries, too.

My breakthrough intention that led me to be bold and unafraid proved to be a guiding light that strengthened my spine, steadied my mind, and sustained me in the months that followed. That focused, clear, consistent intention that was understood and enthusiastically accepted by my team and my colleagues set us on a course that truly shifted outcomes around the world.

Intentionality's Highs and Lows

Now that intentionality plays such a major role in my communications and leadership mindset, I look for it in others. It's easy to recognize those who are driven by a singular intention. We see it in their eyes. We hear it in their voices. Their mission is so ever present, they practically reek of it. There is nothing false, no shred of marketing or public relations to them. There are no talking points, only a deeply held belief, a persistent point to make.

Take Bruce Springsteen, who, clad in blue jeans and T-shirts, has dedicated his music to honoring the everyman. Whether it's the driving beat of "Born to Run" or the ballads "The Promised Land" and "The River," each song Springsteen wrote reaches into your memory and reminds you of the tingle of young love, the ache of hard work, the virtues of striving and struggling, the joy of friendship, and the pain of old age. His lyrics narrate the arc of humanity that most everyone travels. He takes listeners to the Jersey Shore and the roadside bar. It's the same story in all his songs. The man is who he is.

Consider Serena Williams. With every move of her muscled body, she is signaling one thing: that she will be the greatest, as defined on her own terms. When the Williams sisters burst onto the tennis scene, most assumed that Venus, with her elegance and cool demeanor of a classic tennis player, would dominate. But stocky, muscular, emotional Serena surpassed her sister and all other competitors. Since she made her professional tennis debut in 1995, Serena has taken twenty-three Grand Slam titles and became the unquestioned greatest women's tennis player of her time. She also turned the sport on its ear with her fashion choices that screamed, "I will not abide by your traditions!" Defiant and rarely defeated, with every swing of the racket Serena spoke volumes.

Williams and Springsteen, two very different people, share an unwavering intentionality that played in their lives like a drum beating a steady backbeat. It gave them a sureness and made them iconic personas, who always remained true to themselves with their central themes never in doubt.

On the other end of the spectrum, lacking in intentionality when he needed it most, is a man I admire, Michael Bloomberg. A savvy entrepreneur, a successful mayor, and an impactful philanthropist, Bloomberg was unable to articulate a captivating rationale for his presidential bid. Filing to run for office in November of 2019, Bloomberg limped in late to the game. He opted not to compete in the early states of Iowa, New Hampshire, Nevada, and South Carolina, banking on a big win on Super Tuesday. He floundered during the debates, unable to express an inspiring vision for his campaign and getting thrown off course by attacks from his competitors. Bloomberg won only American Samoa on Super Tuesday and missed the 15 percent threshold for proportional delegates in several states. It was too bad. A man of his experience, drive, and accomplishment might have made a hell of a president. But, despite spending nearly a billion dollars, he never caught on. His intentionality quotient was zero.

Conversely, one candidate who flourished and found momentum was Mayor Pete Buttigieg who, at thirty-eight, was the youngest in the field. Mayor Pete's signature issue was generational change. In every speech, he displayed that intentionality through his energy and commitment to building a bridge to a new style of American politics. Another communications master is Senator Elizabeth Warren. The former law professor was highly intentional and staked her campaign on a consistent drumbeat of messaging that she would fight corruption and fix what she considered the unfair and broken economic rules.

First prize for clarity and conviction goes to former Vice President Joe Biden who pinpointed the moment he decided to run for the highest office. In what was perhaps the most stirring video to announce a candidacy, Biden recalled that hot August day when he was at his Delaware home and watched with horror as white supremacists marched through Charlottesville, Virginia. Biden was dismayed at President Trump's muddled response that there "were good people on both sides." Armed with moral clarity, Biden hammered home that his bid for the presidency was rooted in a "battle for the soul of our nation." In just three videotaped minutes, Biden made his entire case. No doubts. No hedging. Full-throated clarity.

I have sympathy for Mayor Bloomberg, and anyone who struggles to identify, express, and hold fast to their intentions. It's especially hard today when we are so easily drawn off our focus. Multitasking is intention's great disabler. I'm guilty of it. I'm fixing dinner while I'm talking on the phone. I'm covertly checking my email while I'm on a Zoom call. I'm bouncing onto Instagram while I'm watching a movie with my family. The multitasking epidemic means we are everywhere and nowhere at the same time. It's devasting to one's ability to think and communicate clearly.

But achieving clarity is what intentional communications demands. As writers, speakers, or advocates, we must be able to easily answer the first question: *What am I really trying to say?*

In 2019, New York Women in Communications honored me with the Matrix Award, one of the highest accolades for communicators. In all candor, over decades, I longed for this award because it signals recognition by one's peers. Having been passed over many times, I let go of my wish, assuming it would never happen. So I was truly surprised when the call came. Delighted, I began to prepare my acceptance speech. Suddenly, after years of sitting in the audience fantasizing about my acceptance remarks, I didn't know what I wanted to say. I wrote several versions and asked my wife, Robin, to read them. She'd finish, look me in the eye, and say, "You can do better." And I knew she was right.

My comments were all over the map with no singular, galvanizing point. I thought about the audience, many aspiring young women, some of whom were on scholarship to communications programs. The more I was able to channel their interest, the clearer my speech goal became. In my opening, I admitted that there was "something I kept secret, a trait I wasn't sure I could be proud of. I was *ambitious*, hungry really for more." I chose to speak about ambition, sometimes a taboo topic, especially for women. Ambition is often derided as an ugly trait. Ambitious people are criticized as land-grabbers concerned only with securing larger and larger empires. I don't agree. For me, ambition is about so much more than steps up the corporate ladder. Rather, it's an honest expression of the mountains one wishes to climb.

In the few minutes I had on stage, I told brief anecdotes about how I channeled my ambition and closed with, "Let me say one thing to the scholarship recipients here today. I urge you to answer from the depths of your heart and the height of your own ambition the question posed by my favorite poet Mary Oliver: 'Tell me, what is it you plan to do with your one wild and precious life?' We are watching with great excitement."

I walked from the stage feeling complete, less so for having won a Matrix and more so for feeling I'd conveyed a point that mattered. My intention was to debunk the negativity that surrounds ambition. I said what I really wanted to say.

Recently, I've made it a habit to locate and land my intention before all communications, including those as basic as a phone call or an email. When older relatives phone, I try to be attentive and present. When I talk to my daughter, I focus on being helpful and nonjudgmental. When I talk to journalists, I seek to be honest and enlightening. If a colleague reaches out, I try to be generous and resourceful. It's not always easy, but it is worth the effort to have this kind of intentional clarity with each exchange. Conversations end on a more positive note for everyone.

This exercise of focused intention is a bit like a yoga position I enjoy, tree pose. Some days, I stand at the front of my mat, shift my weight onto one leg, lift the other, tucking that foot against my thigh. When it all goes right, I find a visual spot in the distance for steadiness, my focus and concentration deepen, I'm strong and balanced, feeling rooted and liberated. In those moments of confidence, I feel as though I could stand in tree pose forever. Other times, I can't find the equipoise, my lifted leg drops, balance is elusive, and I nearly topple over. And then, I try again. Tree pose, like intention claiming, is that easy and that hard.

Whenever you have something important to convey, set a clear and bold intention for that narrative. Land that intention deep within you. Write it down. Scribble it in your journal. Put it on a sticky note and post it on the refrigerator. Print it on a T-shirt or bumper sticker. Say it aloud. Tell others to make that pledge public. Own it.

CHAPTER TWO

Sticking Your Neck Out

Muster the Courage for Candor

I WAS TWENTY-FIVE IN THE SUMMER OF 1986, WORKING IN Washington, DC, as a legislative correspondent in a senator's mailroom. I was fortunate that my first job gave me a chance to explore my fledgling interests in writing and politics. Everything was going well except for one not-so-small detail about me that I hadn't disclosed to the most important people in my life, my parents. I'd been preparing to make this disclosure for several years, maybe since I was a girl. There was a 100 percent chance of the talk going badly; it was only a question of *how* badly. I practiced my lines as I commuted by foot along DC's downtown sidewalks to and from work on Capitol Hill. I rehearsed in front of the mirror above my bathroom sink as I brushed my hair. Staring at my scared self in that mirror, I tried to arrange my face to appear confident, yet empathetic. No one would be fooled. I was terrified.

Would my parents ever speak to me again? Might I be cast out from my family? How would this one data point about me change everything my parents believed to be true about my character? Whatever the cost, my days of deceit had run their course. I was an adult, and I wished to be the truthful, whole person of integrity that my parents had brought me up to be.

"Hey, I'm coming home. I want to talk to you both about something important," I said over the phone to my folks. Even then, I was a polite communicator. I wanted to send a clear signal that this was a meaningful visit. Brace for impact!

I booked a Trans World Airlines flight to St. Louis the following day. I grew up in the heart of the Midwest, a bastion of perceived provincialism. It's a not-very-funny joke that whenever you meet someone from St. Louis, the first thing they ask you is, "Where did you go to high school?" Among native St. Louisans, it's as if all your life determinants, your prospects, and limitations were tied to that single educational coordinate. Those who were enrolled in Parkway West High School would likely marry and have children early. Clayton High Schoolers had the highest chances of success. Kids like me who went to Ladue Horton Watkins High School were deemed privileged and lazy. During my high school years, I fit that descriptor more than I wish to admit. It wasn't until I graduated from college and took my first steps into the working world that I began to find my footing.

On the day I traveled home, I handed my ticket to the gate attendant, boarded the plane, found my window seat near the rear of the plane, sat down, buckled up, and passed out. I have no memory of the flight. Drunk with anxiety, I fell into a deep sleep.

"Ladies and gentlemen, welcome to St. Louis Lambert Field." The attendant's voice over the plane's public address system jolted me awake just as the aircraft's wheels screeched on touchdown.

My dad picked me up at the airport. After he tossed my bag in the trunk, we headed out of the airport to start the twenty-minute drive home. He asked a few questions about work and politics, our shared interests. Mostly, we rode in silence, the St. Louis Cardinals baseball game playing on the radio. Shortstop Ozzie Smith snagged a line drive.

We pulled up the driveway and entered our house via the kitchen. My mom had dinner on the stove, but I can't recall what we ate. Dinner was a blur of Midwestern niceties.

"Please tell us what you've come to say," Mom said after she and I washed, dried, and put the dishes away. "This is making us tense." Making them tense? I was ready to explode! We sat down in the family room. Mom and me on the sofa. Dad in the armchair.

I began my rehearsed remarks. I had a lengthy preamble about how much I loved them, how much they meant to me, and how I treasured our relationship. It was because of all that, I argued, that the revelation to come was essential if we were to continue to have a close, honest relationship. And then I said it.

"I'm gay."

Two words. Several lives changed.

Though largely accepted now and, in some cases, barely considered newsworthy today, homosexuality was still taboo in the 1980s. At the time, being gay would be a career-ender for teachers, as for those in many other careers. In March of 1986, the Supreme Court affirmed the ruling that allowed teachers to be fired for "advocating, soliciting, imposing, encouraging or promoting public or private homosexual activity in a manner that creates a substantial risk that such conduct will come to the attention of school children." In October of that same year, New York City mayor Ed Koch asked the American Legion's Veterans Day parade to allow gay veterans to march. Mayor Koch was ignored. No gay vets would be holding their heads high, squaring their shoulders, and stepping proudly down Fifth Avenue. Nope, not even if the mayor requested it.

Many people were fearful of and angry at gay people because AIDS was in full force. As irrational as that was, it was the reality on the ground. Even at twenty-five, I'd already lost several friends to the cruel epidemic and attended far too many funerals. With no support from the government or medical community in sight, the gay community felt abandoned. During those dark days, many gay people still chose to live in the closet. My parents didn't believe they knew any gay people . . . at least until that evening.

It's against that backdrop that I knew what would come next.

My parents ran to their emotional corners. My mother fumed and my father wept. She was angry and he was sad. She looked away and he stared.

"I am shocked," Dad said, "and I knew it all the time." I had the presence of mind not to argue the seeming inconsistency of his statement in that moment. I let it wash over me.

This man was one of the people I admired most in the world. He was the tallest tree in the forest of the dads. I worried over whether the hurricane of my revelation would cause the limbs of his love for me to merely bend, or to snap off.

"You will never have a spouse, children, or a career!" Dad bellowed, as if being gay was a choice I had made and not a fact from birth.

I don't believe he intended to hurt me with those words. I'll allow that was a parent's fear talking. Fear for me. But those words seared me, shaped me. The intense pain of hearing them shot through me like a sharp arrow and helped forge my life plan—a plan I hadn't clearly articulated before. The candor, mine and theirs, was crystallizing. If I made it out of that family visit in one piece I was, dammit, going to have exactly that: a spouse, a child, and a career. Within that cauldron of candor, I claimed my own life. I'm so grateful.

Why am I telling you this story? No, you didn't mistakenly pick up this book in the business section only to find it was meant to be on the LGBTQ+ shelves. The larger point is that candor is worth it, whatever "it" is for you. You earn respect; you show regard for the other person, even if they do not like what you are saying—perhaps especially if you know your words will not be warmly received. You take the chance because you are willing to suffer short-term consequences for longer-term gains in trust-building. You demonstrate bravery and are rewarded with peace and pride.

I wasn't the only one. Coming-out stories poured from brave souls during this era. It turned out that 1986 was an auspicious time for what was still known then as the Gay Pride movement. Six New York friends seeking a visual shorthand to express their outrage at the government's silence around the AIDS epidemic created a poster with the phrase, "silence = death." That slogan was later adopted by AIDS Coalition to Unleash Power (ACT UP) as one of its main visual references. It was plastered on billboards, printed on bumper stickers and T-shirts. These words weren't just hyperbole. It was a call to action. Failure to agitate and advocate would result in more young men dying. This powerful phrase raised awareness and saved lives.

Just two years later, the United States first celebrated National Coming Out Day, with its emphasis on the most basic form of activism being coming out to family, friends, and colleagues, and living life as an openly gay person. These candid expressions were at the heart of the fast, fierce gay civil rights movement. Our liberation was won one intimate conversation at a time.

I'm amazed at my incredibly good fortune to live during this period of rapid social change for the LGBTQ+ community. Reflecting on it now is like watching a glorious slideshow of progress: the police raid at the Stonewall Inn that ignited protests and demonstrations in 1969; the American Psychiatric Association removing homosexuality from its list of mental disorders in 1973; Harvey Milk, the first openly gay man elected to political office in 1978; Ellen DeGeneres saying "Yep, I'm Gay" on the cover of *Time* magazine in 1997; the US Supreme Court decriminalizing same-sex sexual conduct in 2003; Barack Obama, the first sitting US president publicly supporting LGBTQ+ marriage in 2012; and Mayor Pete Buttigieg campaigning for president and ultimately being named the first openly gay cabinet member in 2020. Those are just the tops of the waves of an ocean of change. This extraordinary social, civic, and political transformation was rooted in candor and truth-telling.

After many years of inching back toward one another, tearful moments, and mutual growth, I have a deep and meaningful relationship with my parents. They are close to me, love my wife and daughter, and are very proud of my career. Today, my parents are among my staunchest supporters, and if you have five minutes—or five hours—they would be pleased to elaborate on my accomplishments!

I'll venture as far as to say that being gay—and open about it—accelerated my professional success. Entering the office having an examined life, and the chutzpah to be vulnerable and honest, cleared the pathway to forge strong, authentic relationships. I no longer had to manage my pronouns when talking about my partner or look over my shoulder in a Gay Pride parade. I was free to bring my entire self to the office and put all my energy into my work.

Celebrity stylist Andrew Gelwicks's book, *The Queer Advantage: Conversations with LGBTQ+ Leaders on the Power of Identity*, backs up my point. Growing up in a conservative part of Ohio, Gelwicks describes living in two pieces: a public side where he pretended to care about the Cincinnati Reds baseball team, and a private side where he belted *Wicked*'s "Defying Gravity" at the top of his lungs, broomstick in hand, really hitting that high end note. Over time, he was able "to see the clear lineage of how my strongest qualities and assets clearly could be linked to those early, often painful times surrounding my grappling with my queer identity."[1]

Gelwicks, a breakthrough communicator himself, conducted a series of interviews with trailblazers and glass-ceiling breakers from athletes to chief executives and from comedians to politicians, all of whom are living their lives supercharged by the freedom found outside the closet. I'm honored to be included among those Gelwicks profiled in his book. I tell my coming-out and gay stories in hopes that it can be of some comfort or inspiration to others.

Coming out is a process one never completes. The work is never done. There's always the new neighbor who's just moved in next door, the boss at the new job, the teacher at your kids' school. Coming out is a lifelong communications exercise. Each time I take a deep breath and hope my candor strikes the right chord.

Candor Warrior: Molly Jong-Fast

I respect candor in others because it signifies courage and clarity. Candor often comes from the unexpected voices. Recently, I heard a clarion call to support science from a layperson and participant in our Covid-19 vaccine clinical trial.

I'm ashamed to admit that, pre-Covid crisis, I didn't think much about clinical trial volunteers. Sure, they existed somewhere in the recesses of my mind. I knew they were critical to the human studies necessary to develop a medicine or vaccine, but I never fully appreciated that these people raise their hands and risk their health without financial reward or recognition.

That changed on September 17, 2020, when the *New York Times* ran an opinion piece by Molly Jong-Fast under the headline, "I Am Not a Brave Person. I Am Also Patient 1133," and the subhead, "Never did I expect to have a calling. Then came the pandemic." According to this compelling first-person account, Molly was enrolled in the trial at Yale New Haven Hospital and inspired by the statistics of rising vaccine hesitancy. "I knew I had to do my part to help create a safe vaccine," she wrote.

With this opinion piece, Molly drew back the heavy curtain of anonymity that cloaked clinical trials. She broke tradition. She refused to be faceless. She was willing to be publicly vulnerable and, in doing so, revealed herself to be courageous. I was in awe. I made it a point to meet her.

Molly wasn't hard to find. She's a celebrated author and pundit as a contributing writer at the *Atlantic* and the author of its newsletter, *Wait, What?* She's written two novels and a memoir. Molly is a regular contributor to *Playboy, Glamour,* and the *Bulwark,* and former editor-at-large at the *Daily Beast.* She has huge followings on Twitter and Instagram and an edgy podcast, *The New Abnormal.* Molly is a one-woman communications juggernaut.

Two months after Molly's opinion piece ran in the *New York Times,* we met in the lobby of Pfizer's headquarters. She strode in, her long red hair flowing. She wore a maxi skirt, motorcycle boots, and a leopard print jacket. The pandemic rules were still in effect, so we both wore masks and bumped elbows in greeting. That began a friendship, and it was my chance to explore why she spoke out about the clinical trial and how she became a breakthrough communicator.

"As soon as I knew about the pandemic, I wanted to be in a vaccine trial. We needed this vaccine to get us out of the pandemic and we're in one of the most anti-science times since the Dark Ages. So, if this vaccine worked—and I prayed it would—I wanted to use my platform to help. I wanted to tell my story to as many people as possible to show it was safe, to normalize medical trials for scientific achievement," Molly explained.

I complimented Molly because her opinion piece did just that. "Thanks, I felt I did something good for the discourse," she replied.

I then asked her where she finds the courage to write on so many intimate subjects including addiction, family turmoil, and politics. Molly's answer surprised me. "Look, I got sober when I was nineteen, and one of the key things about sobriety is that you use your experience to help other people. And you don't tell people to do things that you are unwilling to do yourself. For me, it was very helpful to see how I could draw on my experiences in the clinical trial to help others," she said.

Wow. The courage to speak up and connect with candor can come from any direction. I admire Molly and people like her who are direct, respectful, but don't stand on ceremony when it comes to telling the truth.

The Courage to Stick Your Neck Out

I've had my eye on restaurateur Danny Meyer since I was a kid. He was the cute, older brother of my friend Tommy Meyer. We all grew up in the leafy suburb of Clayton, Missouri. Danny and Tommy's father was the proprietor of two hotels and a French bistro, and their mother was the co-owner of a contemporary art gallery. In our neighborhood, those credentials made the Meyers local celebrities.

Danny built on that legacy of cuisine and culture by opening Union Square Cafe in New York City in 1985 at age twenty-seven. That early success led to a string of award-winning restaurants including Gramercy Tavern, Shake Shack, The Modern, Marta, and many more. He also is a giant in business as the founder of Union Square Hospitality Group. Danny is so celebrated that he is known in many foodie circles and business enclaves and among the New York elite simply as Danny. Like Cher or Prince, no surname required. But the reason I'm including Danny here has nothing to do with food or fame.

Danny has a moral authority that gives him agency in all matters of civic discourse; he has the courage of his convictions and is willing to take risks that have the potential for customer loss. More often than not, however, doing the right thing and standing up for what you believe in has a tremendous payoff.

During his career, Danny has spoken out on many far-ranging topics. I asked him why he has been outspoken on social and policy issues ranging from hunger to nonsmoking and, more recently, to the minimum wage debate and vaccine requirements.

Danny's answer dated back to his early days as a restaurateur. "Sometime soon after I opened Union Square Cafe, I was bemoaning a negative restaurant review to my maternal grandfather," he explained. "He reminded me that I had chosen to go into a public-facing business and that people were going to say a lot of things—some good and some awful—about my business and me. He told me that I needed to know where my center is and stick to it. When you know something is right, you have to do it."

"The first time I stuck my neck out was when we decided to become a no-smoking restaurant in 1990," he said.[2] This made him an early and vocal adapter of no-smoking policies. "It was emotional for me. I'd been mediating arguments between smoking and nonsmoking guests in the restaurant. I'd go home smelling like a cigarette. And my father died of lung cancer. So, I took a stand and banned smoking. I faced a lot of blowback from state and national restaurant associations who claimed no one would come to my restaurant. Even though the move pissed off a lot of people, I did the right thing for my company. Our true north is always what we believe is in the best interest of our employees, our guests, and our community—in that order. In the end, we were busier than ever with guests who appreciated the policy," Danny said. Thirteen years after Danny first banned smoking in his establishment, in 2003, a ban on smoking in New York City restaurants became law.[3]

More recently, in a *Washington Post* Live broadcast, Danny advocated for the Covid relief bill and the raising of the minimum wage in phases. He was among the first in the summer of 2021, when the Delta variant threatened to reverse the progress made by the vaccines to reopen society, to require both employees and customers who wanted to work or dine indoors to show proof of vaccination. "I feel a strong responsibility, on our part as business leaders, to take care of our team and our guests, and that's what I'm doing," Danny said on CNBC's *Squawk Box* on July 29. Danny is a one-man leading indicator of where business leadership is heading.

Showing this kind of courage and candor takes guts—after all, many potential employees and customers could be turned off by this requirement, and he could lose business because of it. On the other hand, it gives others the wherewithal to speak out and up, too. Many business leaders did end up requiring their employees to vaccinate, but Danny was out front insisting that his customers did, too. He wanted to keep his team safe. He announced this policy on CNBC, *CBS Mornings*, and several other outlets. He received a spree of great press. Six days later, New York City mayor Bill de Blasio followed, saying that proof of vaccination would be required for most indoor activities, including dining. That's the power of courage and candor.

In late December 2021, Danny took another bold step, requiring both employees and diners to have a booster shot against the virus in order to work or eat at all Union Square Hospitality restaurants. He laid it out directly for reporters and their audiences. "Hospitality is a team sport—it's kind of like putting on a play on Broadway or playing a basketball game," the restaurateur said. "If you can't field a full healthy team, you're going to have to hit pause."[4]

Courageous Conversation for Taboo Topics

In the summer of 2020, we witnessed the horrific murder of George Floyd. It was so brutal as to almost defy description. Who among us will ever forget the image of a man, facedown and handcuffed, while one officer of the law knelt on his neck until his life was snuffed out and two other officers stood by and looked away? George Floyd's tragedy seared the minds of many Americans, me included. It happened during the pandemic, when we were locked down and not distracted by running errands, shuttling kids to school, or rushing to meetings. The world was still, our newsfeeds were in front of us, and one could not turn away from the painful reality of the institutional racism and nonchalant violence in our country.

In the days that followed, corporations and other institutions convened many townhalls. We held one at Pfizer and I was invited to join a panel of senior executives who met with the company's Global Black Community leadership. All of us on the panel prepared remarks and reviewed materials and rehearsed. I was nervous. I didn't feel my comments were right. They felt forced, flat, and defensive. I asked a couple of colleagues to listen as I prepared. One member of my team, Dr. Dara Richardson-Heron, our chief patient officer and a prominent African American doctor, had the courage to tell me to throw away the remarks. "Speak from the heart," she said, and encouraged me to make it a dialogue.

I took Dara's advice and simply shared my feelings, asked a few questions, and along with other leaders, opened a dialogue. How were my colleagues feeling? We shared hopes for what this moment might yield. How might I help? The conversation changed the temperature on the call from what could have been a frosty monologue to a warm talk. I heard positively from many Black colleagues in the days that followed. Clearly, Dara was right. When in doubt, we should choose candor.

Robert Livingston, a Harvard Kennedy School faculty member, is a leading expert on racism, its causes, and productive avenues to begin the work of anti-racism. In his book, *The Conversation: How Seeking and Speaking the Truth about Racism Can Radically Transform Individuals and Organizations*, Livingston says, "Social change requires social exchange." He has encouraged and facilitated conversations on racism for some of the country's top corporations. Livingston has rules for increasing the likelihood of a productive conversation that include gathering the facts, affirming people to make them feel safe, focusing on the problem and not the person, and finally, showing interest, not animosity. You will never have a meaningful conversation if people feel defensive or ill-prepared.

Livingston's rules make great sense to me. I've tried to put them in practice and added a few of my own:

- *Commit to active listening.* If you're willing to be honest, you have to be willing to accept the return ball. Listen for understanding, not to prepare your response or rebuttal. Take time to respond thoughtfully, not merely react.

- *Do not be ashamed of vulnerability.* Candor doesn't mean you're devoid of feelings. Let people know how you're feeling; that it's tough. They may cut you some slack. It's natural to be uncomfortable in stressful moments. By allowing yourself to be unguarded, you are open to more possibilities.

- *Cocreate solutions.* Candor is only effective if you make it safe for everyone involved, and one way of doing that is including them in finding fixes to the issues raised. It also relieves you of carrying the burden of having all the right answers. There may be no easy solutions in the moment. A remedy conceived of, and supported by, many has a greater chance of success.

There's one rule I've thrown out. It's an old one pulled from etiquette books that insist that the topics of religion, politics, and money are to be avoided in polite company. I don't agree. That's old-fashioned and small-minded. I don't think any relationship is improved by tiptoeing around sensitive topics. Indeed, modern times demand that breakthrough communicators address these and other taboo topics, which also include gender and identity. We have to find a way to address income and social inequalities, religious differences and requirements, and ideological disputes, while remaining respectful and sympathetic.

Corporate Candor Is Not an Oxymoron

Courage and candor are not for individuals only. Companies can also practice brave communications. The most compelling corporate communications are those that express the true depths of a company's character. They knock down barriers and invite the customer in.

People of a certain age might remember Frank Perdue, CEO of Perdue Farms, one of the largest chicken-producing companies. He promoted his company through high-profile advertising, featuring himself on television with the tagline, "It takes a tough man to make a tender chicken." This was revolutionary in the early 1970s, when CEOs were not typically spokespeople for their companies. *Advertising Age* ranked the commercial as one of the best campaigns of the year. In many subsequent versions of the commercial, Perdue encouraged customers to voice any complaints or dissatisfaction with his chickens. At the end of the spots, Perdue said, "Say whatever you have to say; I can take it." That chicken man had courage.

One recent example is tennis superstar Naomi Osaka and the salad company Sweetgreen. Just weeks after Osaka had signed as an endorser of the company's healthy food as a form of self-care, she withdrew suddenly from the French Open citing her mental health. "The truth is that I have suffered long bouts of depression since the US Open in 2018 and I've had a really hard time coping with that," Osaka said. According to the *Wall Street Journal*, Osaka's manager gave Sweetgreen only an hour's notice. I can imagine the scramble behind the scenes at Sweetgreen and the questions it must have been grappling with. This was the young company's first big endorsement, and it was in uncharted waters.

The response by Sweetgreen cofounder and chief brand officer Nathaniel Ru showed how the celebrity-company dynamic had evolved for the better. Rather than tearing up the contract with Osaka, Ru said, "We were really moved by the vulnerability of it and how honest it was." Fainter hearts might have bailed. But the Sweetgreen team then drew closer to the struggling athlete, praised Osaka, and expressed their pride in her for standing up for her beliefs. The Osaka and Sweetgreen alliance is a testimonial to the power of courage and candor in action.

Another example is the accounting company Pricewaterhouse-Coopers's (PwC) response to a mistake made on prime-time television that was seen around the world: the wrong movie was announced as the Best Picture at the 2017 Oscars. PwC, which was tasked with counting the votes, was responsible for the mistake. Instead of making excuses, the firm owned its mistake and offered a short and clear apology. The statement briefly explained what happened, apologized to the people involved, and was gracious in thanking the people who handled the situation. Instead of drawing out an embarrassing situation, PwC took ownership, apologized, and moved on.

Not all corporate communications stories have such happy endings. Many companies frequently fail to put themselves in their best light. They garble communication in acronyms and jargon. The unwillingness to speak candidly leads to foggy, bureaucratic corporate speak.

With over three decades in corporate America, I'm fluent in this language. For example, assume you are discussing a pending big decision and you ask when it might occur and the response is, "We will cross that bridge when we come to it." You can bet that it will never happen. Why not just say that? Or, if you are discussing something complex and someone asks a clarifying question and the answer is, "This is a paradigm shift." You can rest assured no one really understands what's happening. Why not admit as much? People will likely relate. Finally, when a bruising assessment is offered and the recipient says, "Thank you for the feedback," I imagine what he really means is "screw you."

I've waged a war against corporate speak. I've made it my business to try to rid my colleagues of this annoying habit. My team will tell you that I redline and return memos, send back speeches for rewrites, and rip up press releases if the language is couched in corporate clichés or legalese. Those of us who communicate on behalf of companies have a duty to reject empty, bureaucratic language and connect with clarity. No, you can't always reveal certain information to everyone;

that is the nature of business. You cannot go rogue and hurt the company and its people, shareholders, and others who may be impacted by indiscretion (a topic I address later). But you can be clear about what you know and what you don't know, and that some information cannot be shared at a particular moment but will be when the time is right. You owe stakeholders that respect.

I had the chance to put this straight-talk theory into action in the fall of 2020. Like many fellow Americans, I watched the first presidential debate between President Trump and former Vice President Joe Biden. I was cross-legged on the sofa with a bowl of popcorn at my side, anticipating the punches and counterpunches that were sure to fly. What I didn't expect was that in the first five minutes of the debate, President Trump said that he talked to Pfizer and intimated that he had inside information that the vaccine could be available sooner than what was being reported.[5]

In shock, I jumped off the couch, sending my popcorn flying. I started texting my boss, Albert Bourla. *Did he just say that?* We were stunned to find ourselves caught in the crossfire of the US presidential debate.

Perhaps we shouldn't have been so surprised. As the fall approached and the public was anticipating the Covid-19 vaccine readout coming in proximity to the election, the vaccine was becoming politicized. Some loud voices wanted us to move faster, while others begged us to go slower, all in the name of partisan politics. For months, we'd been standing our ground and refusing to allow ourselves to be pulled into the political vortex. The vaccine was for everyone, no matter their political leanings.

"What should we do?" Albert asked. We discussed our options and decided to write an opinion piece for publication in a major newspaper. I stayed up late into the night drafting, and the next day Albert and I edited it back and forth. I submitted it for publication to the *New York Times*, *Washington Post*, *USA Today*, and others. Indignant by having been made a political tool, I felt certain our carefully reasoned, science-based argument would catch an editor's eye. One by one, these outlets rejected our submission. Why? Were our facts not compelling? Were our arguments weak? No. The reason for rejection was that we were trying to lower the temperature, deescalate the situation. That doesn't sell newspapers. Several editors were as brazen to say they would print our piece if we were willing to sling some mud at President Trump. Of course, we would not. In the end, we chose to share Albert's letter with our Pfizer employees and post it on our website. Here's an excerpt:

> Now, we are approaching our goal and despite not having any political considerations with our pre-announced date, we find ourselves in the crucible of the U.S. Presidential election. In this hyper-partisan year, there are some who would like us to move more quickly and others who argue for delay. Neither of those options are acceptable to me. Against this backdrop, people need to know three things:
>
> First, we are moving at the speed of science. With a virus this ferocious, time is our enemy. This week, we will hit the grim marker of 1 million deaths globally and the number continues to climb. This danger supersedes any other timing considerations.
>
> Second, we would never succumb to political pressure. The only pressure we feel—and it weighs heavy—are the billions of people, millions of businesses and hundreds of government officials that are depending on us. We've engaged with many elected leaders around the globe through this health crisis, but Pfizer took no investment money from any government. Our independence is a precious asset.
>
> Third, our priority is the development of a safe and effective vaccine to end this pandemic. I have a duty to Pfizer's 171-year history to honor our legacy of discovering and manufacturing high-quality medicines. We will never cut a corner. Pfizer's purpose is simple: "Breakthroughs That Change Patients' Lives." It's our North Star.

To my amazement, the letter got a ton of pickup on social media, broadcast news, and print. More than 100,000 people viewed the letter across our social channels. Not only were we discovering a vaccine, but we were creating a content machine, too. From that point forward, I no longer prostrated myself in front of the media begging them to print opinion letters. We posted everything on our website and let it fly. Our declaration of independence was heard around the world . . . and with that I learned about the power of pure conviction.

My advice to leaders everywhere, whether you're running a small nonprofit or leading a *Fortune* 100 company, is to never underestimate the power of your own pen. A heartfelt letter to employees and stakeholders on any topic from racism to climate change, from minimum wage to inflation, will carry great weight as long as it's candid and courageous.

Be Ready to Be on Candor's Receiving End

"You'd better sit down." Whenever anyone says this to me, I feel more like throwing up. That's what my boss said as he was about to give me the results of a 360-degree feedback exercise. This was at American Express Company and early in my private-sector career. It was my first exposure to 360-degree feedback. For the uninitiated in this human resources practice, it is an employee review method whereby input is gathered from the employee's subordinates, colleagues, and supervisor through anonymous surveys. A self-evaluation is also part of the package. It's a tool that lays bare what others think of you and how that compares with your own self-assessment.

I took a chair and felt sweat rise on my upper lip. My boss read through what my subordinates had to say. I barely listened as he cruised through my "strengths" and waited for the hammer to drop. He then came to what is euphemistically referred to as the "development opportunities." That's corporate speak for "things at which you really suck." Many of my colleagues thought I "managed up," meaning that I cared more about what my bosses thought than what they thought. Ouch. It was painful to hear. Maybe because it was true.

If I was going to practice candor, I could not be surprised or offended when it was practiced *on* me—especially since I was in a position to advocate it to others. Anyone in any leadership or management position should model and encourage truth-telling. Even though I know this intellectually, I felt humiliated. I let the criticism sink in. I didn't try to defend myself. Instead, I asked for specific examples of times I had managed up so that I could learn from them.

As I reflected on what I heard, I had to come to terms with what insecurities had caused me to behave that way and why. I grew up in a house where I was encouraged to show my parents how knowledgeable I was about my schoolwork and current events. I won praise and, I thought, love (although my parents loved me no matter what) by showing my mother and father that I was smart. I managed up to them. I carried that with me to my job and, in the process, lost sight of the most important people of all, my team.

I have never forgotten that criticism, and I try to be conscious of it as a manager and a leader. In the decades that followed, I worked and continue to work hard not to be that person. I'm certain I don't always succeed, but I make the effort. I encourage those around me to speak up when they see my management style veering up so I can bring it down a notch or two.

Encourage those around you to be candid, and welcome it. If you fly off the handle, you're going to destroy the trust between colleagues. The downside of that is huge; your people are going to be afraid to tell you things you need to know. Isolation is a grave danger to leaders.

One Last Argument for Courage and Candor

You never know when you'll never have another chance. When the words of an apology are forever lodged in your throat because you fear the hurt is too deep. When the love letter dies in your draft file because the risk of rejection seems too great. When the outreach to an estranged family member is never extended because the breach feels too wide. Close that gap.

Don't hesitate. Have courage and let candor be your lifeblood. Deliver it with care and respect. Be brave. Have the guts and the know-how to cut through the clutter of our noisy world by being direct, calm, and approachable. Stand for something. Take risks with bold declarations. Listen. Do what's required to be forthright. Speak truth to power. Believe in straight talk. Know that candor makes us stronger and that, in some cases, it can even save lives.

CHAPTER THREE

Am I Boring You?

Stay Curious, Be Creative

AS A YOUNG WOMAN, I WAS NOT A GREAT TRAVELER. I WAS happiest at home, in my furry slippers, enjoying leftovers on the couch in front of my favorite television shows. Curiosity for me often went no further than the latest must-see cable series. A stack of movies and a cozy blanket was my idea of nirvana. Even into full-blown adulthood, watching repeats of *The Sopranos* or *Sex and the City* was my idea of weekend plans.

All that changed in 2000 when Estée Lauder Companies named me chief communications officer and its legendary vice chair, Jeanette Sarkisian Wagner, became my mentor, kicking my lethargic ass in the process.

Early in my tenure, I was assigned to an overseas business trip to Beijing with Jeanette. Driven and opinionated, a visionary and perfectionist, Jeanette was revered for having built the cosmetic giant's lucrative international beauty business. I appreciated that it was an honor to accompany her to China. With her blazing intellect and an appetite for hard work, I also knew traveling alongside Jeanette would be a grueling journey with a packed schedule. There would be no time for deep soaks in the hotel bathtub, let alone end-of-day TV watching.

Near the conclusion of our first day in Beijing, after back-to-back meetings, Jeanette and I headed back to our hotel—or so I thought. I was starting to fade and looking forward to collapsing in my room. No such luck. Jeanette turned to me and said, "We need to get out and see something real." She grabbed a street map, took me by the hand, and declared, "Explore the new!" Jeanette had a philosophy for traveling: forget the comfortable, the easy, and the expected; go in search of the new, the local, and the real.

Within the hour, we were at the Red Gate Gallery, a recently opened contemporary art gallery abutting the historic Great Wall. The gallery was an old guard post that had been refurbished. Only a few paintings were displayed in this dramatic space, but it pulsed with energy. The modern art scene in China was emerging from the shadows of a restricted past, and the very presence of this art space, alongside ancient and iconic architectural achievements, was symbolic of "the new." I left the Red Gate Gallery with a small painting and a large appreciation for treasures—physical and spiritual—that can be found on the road. I was in awe.

The next day, following hours spent in marketing meetings and sales reviews, Jeanette asked, "Do you have dinner plans?"

Was she joking? I knew no one in Beijing, or anywhere in China for that matter. I was dreaming of a hamburger delivered to my door from room service, but I knew that wasn't the right answer. I shrugged my shoulders. "Come with me," she said, again literally dragging me by the hand. We ended up at the house of one of her Chinese chums for dinner. This worldly gentleman hosted us for dim sum in the center courtyard of his traditional home. Like Jeanette, her friend had grown up in the magazine business, was an intrepid traveler, and a night owl.

Despite my exhaustion, I learned a great deal about Chinese culture, including the history of the imperial architectural style of his home and the usefulness of the medicinal herbs in his garden—beauty and utility bound together in one man's abode. My horizons were widened. The dialogue was far ranging as both Jeanette and her friend had lived and worked in many countries. They told me of their business conquests, how they took a machete to red tape, forged through thickets of bureaucracies, and celebrated victories with champagne. As they reminisced under the starlight sky, my own curiosity was aroused, my exhaustion replaced by wonder. I could have stayed all night.

"Dear, jet lag is boring," Jeanette said to me at the end of the evening. Point taken.

No, this book is not a travel guide. The point is not geographic, but psychographic. This fierce Armenian woman, a former journalist, editor, and groundbreaking businesswoman, showed me by example how to cultivate my curiosity, venture off the beaten path, find new perspectives, question the unknown, and by extension, improve my communications skills. Huh? You may be asking what does wandering have to do with writing? How does curiosity enhance communication? Over years of working and journeying alongside Jeanette, I learned to discover, challenge, and stretch my own boundaries and habits. These qualities made me more attentive, with eyes and ears tuned to new discoveries.

Breakthrough communicators are relentlessly curious. They are interested in things outside themselves, they are virtuoso listeners, and they ask probing questions—and listen mindfully to the answers. At its core, language and word choice, content quality, and platform selection (written, oral, digital, etc.) benefit from the willingness to see life from an original vantage point, and even from being a little wild. Don't settle for dull sentences. Reject lazy language. Season your communications with observations and insights gained on your journeys.

Straying from known or well-traveled paths takes your mind to new places and offers references and perspectives that empower you to be more specific, colorful, and nuanced in your communications. Writer John Steinbeck said, "People don't take trips—trips take people." Let yourself be taken. It will manifest for you in more vivid descriptions, sharper analogies, and more vibrant scene setting. You will have the credibility of your experience and worldliness—something that first trip to China and many other subsequent trips there has given me. Now, at a time when the relationship between the United States and China is strained, I draw on the things I observed on those trips to try to understand and advocate smartly on our bilateral issues ranging from trade restrictions to intellectual policy protections.

Go to the Source

Elizabeth Gilbert wrote in *Big Magic: Creative Living beyond Fear* that following our curiosity enables us to accept uncertainty with a positive attitude, which results in opening our minds to new ideas, skills, and ways of solving problems.[1] I asked Jeanette about the source of her curiosity, the font of her desire to always see more. From where and from whom did she find that determination? Jeanette told me that as a child of an immigrant family in Chicago, she didn't have money to spend on entertainment. The highlight of her day was sitting around the dinner table hearing her family tell stories of their brave passage to the United States, of making their way in a new country, and the value her family placed on education and hard work. Listening night after night to her loved ones share the details of their quotidian dramas— from Armenia and in America—inspired her to lead a robust life, to have adventures to recount and tales to tell.

Hearing Jeanette talk about her parents, I was reminded that my own family had a dinnertime ritual. Every evening, Mom insisted that my kid brother, Billy, and I each bring a news fact to the table, garnered from one of our two local papers, either the conservative morning paper, the *Globe Democrat*, or the evening's liberal alternative, the *Post-Dispatch*. Our job was to inform the family and explain its significance. Billy and I thought this weird at best, and often cruel. Why couldn't we just chat and chow down like other families? Dutifully, and usually just ahead of the dinner bell, we scoured the newspapers, clipped an article (no weather forecasts or sports scores allowed), and did our best to report and analyze our offering. In hindsight, I'm grateful for having learned at an early age to take an interest in the world and contextualize events and express my views about them.

To this day, I try to live up to my family's standard to bring something revelatory to whatever dining table I join. Since my experiences with Jeanette, now when I travel, I fight the urge to collapse on the hotel bed regardless how fluffy the pillows or how high the thread count in the sheets. Rather, I channel my inner Jeanette and push myself to "see something real." It exercises my curiosity muscle. I've made it a firm rule to always push myself and those I'm with to leave the confines of airports, hotels, and conference rooms to immerse in the local culture. In this way, I've discovered historic and cultural treasures, met people I'd otherwise never have known, and often gained an insight or important truth that has helped me communicate in more relatable ways.

Ten years after that Beijing trip, I joined Pfizer and brought my wanderlust with me. Unfortunately, its executives were not inclined to depart from rigid business itineraries. As I had been, they were stuck in corporate mode: attend seminar, sit on panel, tour factory, have business dinner, retreat to hotel room, leave the next day ASAP. I was intent on changing that mindset and injecting some of Jeanette's energetic curiosity into my team. That drive and determination to explore has advanced my career and my effectiveness as a communicator.

One of my first trips with senior leaders from Pfizer was to our warehouse in Memphis, Tennessee. When we finished our work, I hijacked our van and forced a detour to the National Civil Rights

Museum. This small museum was next door to the Lorraine Motel, where Martin Luther King Jr. was shot. Its collection of civil rights memorabilia included Rosa Parks's bus—the very one in which she refused to give up her seat. What a find!

Once I cajoled the team into the museum, I found a guide and organized a quick tour for our group. "Who was Rosa Parks?" asked a young member of the pharma team as we arrived at the museum. My other new colleagues checked their watches. I imagined they wondered who in the hell had hired me. But as our eloquent guide spoke, my colleagues started to perk up and listen, taking a genuine interest in what she was sharing. Ultimately, the visit made a positive impression on the team.

Now several of them stray off course on their business trips, a practice I encourage in them and myself because it sparks useful insights. When I traveled to Ethiopia with my colleagues from the Pfizer Foundation team, at the end of a day spent viewing the health clinics we supported, we didn't all run off to our rooms. The team and I sat together under the stars and wrote our observations and feelings. We shared our stories, and through those notes, we deepened our collective understanding of what we witnessed and drew closer as a group.

Curiosity's Successor: Creativity

Curiosity also opens your mind and allows you to become more creative. Curiosity leads you to learn new things, which helps you see and make new connections between ideas, which is creativity in action. As a process, creativity can feel like a process that many of us mistakenly feel is reserved for more artistic or extraordinarily gifted people. It's not. However, creativity may not come naturally or easily for all of us. The good news is, with deliberate practice and active curiosity, it *can* be learned. It's worth the effort to acquire creative strength to the best of your ability because it makes our communications more vibrant, original, and memorable. It helps us solve problems and see challenges in new ways.

One must commit to creativity. It takes practice. Give it time. Observe its impact. Honor its rituals. Value it as much as any precious resource. Don't let the fostering of creativity and originality take a back seat to the pursuit of wealth or power.

There are several rituals I use to get my creative juices flowing:

- *Wake up early.* Getting up with the hens may be a vestige of my Midwestern upbringing, but it's a tradition I've held to wherever I've lived. I treasure the time to sit quietly, savor the first sips of my coffee, and do a little light journaling. I take notes on what went right—or wrong—the day before. How might I approach today differently? I record my reflections.

- *Scan the news.* I'm a news junkie. I check sources from across the globe, because being informed about current events raises its own set of questions to ponder; it also allows me to connect the dots between events and see a bigger picture. In drawing new connections, new ideas arise. An editorial perspective might form the basis of an executive's speech. Something fashionable in the style section may prompt an idea for a product launch.

- *Move.* On as many days as I can, I take a long, three-mile walk. Moving my body jogs my mind. According to Johns Hopkins Medicine, raising your heart rate has multiple health benefits, including lowering your stress. Stress and anxiety block free and expansive thinking. I also enjoy the solitude of walking. I always carry a small notepad so I can quickly jot down observations as they float into mind. I'm old school, but you can also use a note-taking app on your smartphone. Sometimes I listen to podcasts, but more often I opt for birdsong.

- *Suspend reality.* I allow myself to believe in fortuity. As a young girl, on weekend mornings, I went fishing with Papa, my grandfather. We sat in the flat-bottom boat with a small outdoor motor perfect for trolling around quiet coves in the Lake of the Ozarks. Just before we cast our lines, Papa spat on the minnows that we used for bait. "For luck," he would say and give a wink. To this day, I still stealthily spit on things to raise my chances or improve my odds a bit. On occasion I subvert my Midwestern pragmatism and, for just a moment or two, trust in magical forces.

- *Reserve the time.* I forgo some activities to preserve time for my writing (at least that's my excuse for not going to the gym). One fall weekend, I attended a writing workshop in Stonington, Connecticut, where I joined a small group of writers at various stages of developing their craft. We read poetry aloud, wrote down observations, read one another's work, and bonded. I admired everyone there for taking time from their daily pressures to prioritize their creative projects. But you don't have to travel. On summer evenings, I go no farther than my backyard and delight in the fireflies. When autumn arrives, I marvel at the changes in nature as the leaves turn color and fall to the ground to make way for winter. There is a growing body of research that says spending time in nature and enhanced creativity are connected.[2]

Legendary choreographer Twyla Tharp wrote in *The Creative Habit* about practices that can help us take the first steps of a creative act. One practice that I endorse is something Tharp calls "scratching." "Scratching takes many shapes. A fashion designer is scratching when he visits vintage clothing stores, studies music videos and parks himself at a sidewalk café to see what pedestrians are wearing," Tharp writes. She gives many examples of professionals—film directors, architects, chefs, and others—who draw inspiration from simple acts of scratching, ranging from walking in foreign cities to rummaging through old cookbooks.

With scratching, Tharp demystifies creativity. Thankfully, we need not wait for divine inspiration. Most good ideas build off other ideas. Inspiration is everywhere. In that spirit, I had a wild idea on an overnight transatlantic flight—well, actually, like many original thoughts, mine was a riff on someone else's.

A Senior Intern Experiment

In the spring of 2016, I was on a plane returning home from a business trip in Europe. I was tired, cranky, and well into a glass of mediocre white wine. I guess I was scratching for anything interesting to occupy my time when I scrolled through the little screen in the seat back searching for a movie. I clicked on *The Intern*, starring Robert De Niro as the seventy-year-old intern who works for Anne Hathaway, the young, struggling CEO of a booming startup. De Niro is a wise and lovable intern who offers Hathaway quiet counsel. He bolsters her confidence and rallies the staff. He becomes the office's spiritual leader and Hathaway's best friend.

Halfway through the movie and now deep into my second glass of still mediocre wine, tears were streaking down my face. I wanted some of what Hathaway got from her intern—a mature presence, a true confidant, an office friend.

I knew as soon as the movie's credits rolled that I had to have this, too. As I fidgeted in my airplane seat, I noodled my plan. I was certain that there was only one person who could fill this opening for me. That was Paul Critchlow. He was a communications legend when I was just starting my way up the ladder. When I was a junior member of the American Express public relations team, Paul headed up the same function at Merrill Lynch. When our American Express team huddled to tackle a tough public relations problem, my boss would say, "I'll call Critchlow." It was understood that he'd know what to do. Paul was *the man* in our field.

By the time my plane landed at JFK Airport, my strategy was locked. My first step was to get sign-off from Pfizer's chief human resources officer, Chuck Hill. I worried that Chuck wouldn't agree to my scheme, seeing the prospect of an elderly gentleman for an intern as nuts. Surely, the idea might go very badly or fail altogether. The next morning, I poked my head into Chuck's office and pitched the concept. After a long run-on sentence explaining the idea, I said, "So, what do you think?" Seeing my excitement and determination, Chuck gave me the green light.

Next, could I really ask Paul—a Vietnam veteran, a former journalist and press secretary, an accomplished business executive recently retired—to be my summer intern?

I invited Paul to lunch later that same week. I chose a bistro in the West Village near his apartment. The trees were just starting to sprout green. I arrived early and asked for a table by the window.

Paul sauntered in, looking handsome and relaxed, his silver hair combed back. He was a man who had achieved a lot and was finding himself—maybe for the first time—with time to spare. I hemmed and hawed as we ate. Made small talk.

I waited until our hamburgers were digested to pop the question. "Have you seen the movie *The Intern*?" I asked.

"Nope," Paul replied. I explained the premise. How an older, retired guy joined a company as an intern. That he labored alongside younger workers. That it was tough at first, but, in the end, the intern was a transformative figure to all the office workers—especially to the boss.

"Would you be my summer intern?" My heart was racing.

Paul paused before responding. He touched his ear, and I wondered whether he was checking his hearing aid to be sure he'd heard me right. He took a long draw on the straw bobbing in his Diet Coke. Paul had previously told me that he'd quit drinking years ago—for good reason. Among the things I admired about Paul was his willingness to reveal his shortcomings, to talk about his failings without a blink.

"Interesting," he said. "Let me think about it."

That evening I fretted that Paul might think I was silly . . . or worse that he might be angry that I was trying to lure him from his retirement. What I didn't know then was that retirement was not suiting him—that he was feeling restless, bored, and maybe a little marginalized.

The next day Paul got back to me. He was, in fact, interested.

"I hope you'll share some of your wisdom with our interns," I said.

"I'll probably learn more from them than they will from me."

Paul was onto something. He wasn't showing up with his ego, but with his curiosity. There was lightness to him, an openness that surprised me. Maybe I too could still learn something in this job I'd inhabited for so long. I immediately started to feel more enthusiastic about the possibilities.

"And I hope you'll be my confidential adviser," I said.

"But, of course," he replied.

This role didn't have a standard job description. We both knew what I was talking about: Why it was the special kicker in the deal between us. Why I needed that above all else. This would be Paul's bonus gift to me. How rare to find someone who has walked a mile in your shoes. Paul had worked many years in the same job as me. In our position—leading a corporate communications function for a massive multinational—you see it all. I worked for one CEO who was being hounded by the tabloids for having a child out of wedlock. I was the consigliere to another corner-office occupant who regularly melted down and berated the team. I talked executives off the ledge of incredibly stupid ideas. Paul understood all of that. He'd lived a version of the same story. He could help me.

Then, Paul and I talked terms.

"I'd be happy to pay you a consulting fee," I said.

"What do the other interns make?" Paul asked.

"$18.25 an hour."

"That'll be fine," he said. Money was no longer a driver for him. We both knew we were onto something richer than gold. We were embarking on an intergenerational experiment. Though we are both professional communicators, in that moment, we felt like scientists.

"Well, let me at least give you an office," I said.

"Where do the other interns sit?"

"In a bullpen in the media shop."

"That will be fine," Paul said. The communal table where the college kids sit would be our laboratory. We were pumped!

And so, in the summer of 2016, Paul Critchlow, former vice chairman of Bank of America Merrill Lynch, became my summer intern. On his first day, he waited in line to get his photo taken for his company badge. He attended orientation in the crowded room of newbies. He made friends who were younger than his children. The interns launched him on social media and created a Facebook page for him. "It never ends!" Paul remarked about his social media feed.

Paul taught the other summer interns, leading sessions on topics ranging from "Becoming an Effective, Cool, and Calm Corporate Spokesperson" to "The Vietnam War, My Story." He was imparting priceless gems of wisdom. Sharing, in bite-sized pieces, lessons he'd learned over a lifetime.

Paul's most popular lecture was called "The Power of Failure." I sat in on that class and sighed with relief hearing all the mistakes he'd made. None of us have all the answers.

And like De Niro in the movie, Paul was beloved. He was not only popular among the interns, but the professional staff adored him, too. They jostled for time on his calendar. Seems everyone was looking for exactly what I wanted—someone older and wiser to talk with. A seasoned perspective. An experienced point of view. An empathetic ear.

I felt reenergized and rewarded for my creative risk-taking. We had bucked the "it can't be done here" syndrome. We'd innovated within a big corporation. And we succeeded. It felt like flying.

We connected the communications dots when our experiment in a cross-generational internship went a little viral. In September of that year, *Fast Company* magazine wrote a cover story on Paul titled, "Why a 70-Year-Old Retiree Went Back to Work . . . as an Intern." Initially, the reporter was cynical about the program, thinking maybe it was a public relations ploy. But, like the rest of us, he fell in love with the concept and our senior intern as he learned about him and how he would work with us. *Fast Company* also sent a video crew to shadow Paul for its online edition. This coverage was especially gratifying because, for years, I'd tried without success to position Pfizer for inclusion in *Fast Company*. It was the first time that Pfizer had earned a multipage story in this innovators' magazine, causing people to take a second look at my company.

A few months later, South by Southwest, the massive innovation conference held annually in Austin, Texas, invited Paul and me to speak. There, we not only reveled in our fifteen minutes of fame, but also reintroduced Pfizer to a packed auditorium of young innovators. One rarely gets a chance for a second look, and it appeared that people in the audience liked what they saw in our seventy-year-old intern, his middle-aged boss, and a 167-year-old pharma company that was acting like a startup.

Begin with Inquiry

As children, we are natural questioners. Why is the sky blue? Why is ice cream cold? As we mature, the freedom to ask questions is not as instinctive. We become too self-conscious to ask silly questions. That insecurity often leads us to lower the blinds on our innate inquisitiveness. Sadly, as we grow self-conscious, we grow incurious.

Inquisitiveness is one of the reasons I admire the poet Mary Oliver, who, even in her advanced age, always posed provocative questions. As I wrote in chapter 1, my favorite poem is Oliver's "The Summer Day," which opens with three questions, "Who made the world? Who made the swan, and the black bear? Who made the grasshopper?" Questions open our minds and draw us in.

How can we keep the flame of inquiry alive? One way is to think like a journalist. When I was a reporter for my high school newspaper, my teacher encouraged me to flip open my notebook and start with the basics of the five Ws: who, what, when, where, and why. She taught that these essential facts must be answered in the lead of any story. I was a sportswriter covering routine stuff—a field hockey victory, a football injury, a coach's retirement. I wasn't reeling in Pulitzer prizes, but I was learning a valuable discipline of reporting, investigating, writing, fact-checking, and reviewing. The five Ws gave me a solid grounding. Any aspiring communicator should take a turn at the reporter's wheel. It's hard work and sharpens your skills.

Short of working in journalism, communicators need to build a network of reporters. I don't mean cold-calling reporters or bombarding their email with a pitch, but nurturing relationships over time. Reporters have their finger on the pulse of what's happening across society, have a sharp eye for trends, and are the gatekeepers to what makes its way into the news each day and history over time. Often, when I talk to reporters, I learn more from them than they do from me.

My friend Dan Roth is a good example. I first met Dan in the fall of 2005, when he, as a staff reporter for *Fortune,* reported on the Lauder family. His focus was on the then-third generation that was in charge. I was the chief communicator at Estée Lauder, and a story on the family in an outlet as prestigious as *Fortune* could not be delegated. I handled that one personally, was present at every interview, and sweated every fact-checking detail. There were so many ways this article could go sideways—a family member might be underappreciated, or the delicate balance that keeps a family working together harmoniously in a public company could be upset.

Over weeks of his reportage, I saw that Dan was a conscientious journalist who followed the facts and had a real knack for understanding people. On that basis, I granted him extensive access to our founder's grandchildren, who were in positions of authority in the company. The night before the story ran, I slept very little.

The next morning, when I saw the story in print (as we did in those days), it ran under the headline, "Sweet Smell of Succession: Dynasties don't last forever. But Estée's Lauder's grandkids aren't about to let this beauty empire crumble." This exhaustive profile was a rave review of the family. They were portrayed as the serious, sensitive, committed, and hardworking people that they are. I loved the story. More importantly, the family was happy with the piece. We had a winner.

After his tenure at *Fortune*, Dan held positions of increasing responsibility at several national publications. In the summer of 2011, Dan joined LinkedIn as editor. Today he is its editor-in-chief. I admire Dan and LinkedIn as positive and productive forces in the dynamic conversation on careers. I'm a big LinkedIn fan and scroll through often to follow the ideas of others (online scratching).

I reconnected with Dan to ask him about curiosity. He said, "As a journalist, I ask a million questions. I want to know how everything works. When I arrived at LinkedIn, I was asking tons of questions, meeting with anyone who would see me. It's how I learned my new job." The change from traditional print journalism to the dynamic, career-focused, online forum was dramatic.

He continued, "It's one thing to be curious, it's another thing to use that curiosity to challenge your own beliefs. The industry I came from, print journalism, was top down. I was the editor and I told people what to do. When I got to LinkedIn, and content came from the community, I had a lot to learn—and learned the most by watching how my boss, Ryan Roslansky [now LinkedIn's CEO], got the most out of people. I stopped telling people what to do and started asking questions of senior and junior people. Why are you doing it that way? If we were starting over, is this the way we would do it? What makes you so certain this is the right way?" This wasn't done in an accusatory way but in a truly curious sense of interest.

"The job was really humbling, and I realized I had so much to learn. I found those questions led me to a new place. The dialogue created a shared understanding and a better way to work. People were bought in, not just doing something because the boss told them to," Dan said. What a profound way to communicate and to lead. Dan is considered one of the great thinkers and media leaders, known for his ability to educate, delight, and connect with LinkedIn's growing community and more than 300,000 followers.

Cultivate Your Curiosity and Creativity

Never think you aren't curious or cannot be creative. Never give up on the quest to be original. Build your own creativity practice. My mantras may help.

Live as an abecedarian. If you're not familiar with the term, it means a person who is just learning, a novice, and . . . there, you've discovered something new already. Research shows that trying something for the first time stimulates your brain and gets those synapses firing.[3]

Claudia Slacik was a highly successful business executive who had held senior banking positions at Citigroup and JPMorgan and was the chief banking officer at the Export-Import Bank in the Obama administration. She's also a neighbor and friend whom I admire for her intellectual wanderlust. Claudia is a lifelong learner and was a fellow at Harvard's Advanced Leadership Initiative in 2018 to "find out how people live in the last third of their lives."

"Everyone is born with the capacity to be curious, but some people chase it. I did," Claudia explained. When she was unexpectedly fired from a mid-level job more than two decades ago, Claudia took solace in becoming an abecedarian. With little cooking experience, Claudia enrolled in the French Culinary Institute. As she was growing up, members of her family knew how to make music in the kitchen, but not Claudia. She recalled trying to make veal scallopini for a friend that "tasted like papier-mâché. I was never much of a chef."

Claudia did have a drive to understand how to create flavors. After graduating from the institute, Claudia (who was again gainfully employed as a banker and swears banking is far easier than being a chef) talked her way into a one-night-a-week job at Annie's Breads to do a deep dive into how to make sourdough bread. In the mornings following those nights at Annie's, she brought her freshly baked goods into the office. Her colleagues went crazy for it. They circled her desk in anticipation of the fresh-baked goods. It opened new avenues of dialogue with her peers. So, via sourdough bread, Claudia began a new language rooted in homemade food.

Claudia's foray into the French Culinary Institute gave her a new set of communications tools. "Cooking is my language of love," she said.

So, sign up for a class that interests you, especially one that's outside your comfort zone. There are so many wonderful offerings online at reasonable rates. Your local library is a great place to start. Check out its website for programs, usually free to the public. And if a class is more commitment than you can make, how about a lecture? A quick check on the 92nd Street Y events calendar showed a rich range of choices from "Shakespeare's Developing Sense of Empathy" to "Public Art in America." You don't have to enroll for a degree or even a semester. Start simply with a class that gives you the chance to be a beginner again.

Get under the hood. Go in search of the gritty details. Don't just drive a car, but also seek to understand the engine that makes it run. Don't merely accept things at face value, but also dig for understanding. For example, at The Estée Lauder Companies, all employees are encouraged to take the sales staff training and spend a day behind the counter. I did this once during the busy holiday season. Greeting the bustling shoppers and attempting to connect with customers on the go gave me fresh ideas about how to engage with the public and a new appreciation for how hard it is to be on your feet all day.

Try meeting a new person or talk to someone you don't normally interact with. I'm not suggesting you will find a new best friend, but maybe just an acquaintance with a fresh perspective that can crack open the window of your creativity. Introduce yourself to a neighbor and ask how she came to live next door. Say hello to your barista if he's not too busy and find out how he enjoys serving coffee to the public . . . or not. Greet your mailperson with a smile and see how long she's been delivering on your route and who she's met along the way. The depth of human experience is one of the deepest wells of inspiration.

Read long form. Don't just read social media posts and brief news flashes. Immerse yourself in long-form reading. Find a book that intrigues you, hopefully a hard cover, so you can enjoy the physicality of it. Try something by a first-time author. Lean into fiction. Read a political book that you think you'll disagree with, and maybe you will understand something about human nature or your Uncle Bob, who you always end up arguing with over Thanksgiving dinner. You might even change your mind about something. Reading in depth uses your brain differently and allows you to escape in the very best way. Reading books enhances imagination, expands our world, and allows us to have experiences even if we're sitting on the couch.[4]

As a girl, I devoured the *Little House on the Prairie* series and was transported to the big woods, fascinated by the ways Ma and Pa managed on the great plains and mesmerized by Laura's adventures. I tore through the *Nancy Drew Mystery Stories* as I sought to build my sleuthing skills. Reading stimulated my imagination and let me travel far beyond my childhood bedroom to parts unknown. To this day, I'm never bored if I have a good book in my handbag.

It doesn't take much to set the wheels of imagination in motion. It will not only enhance your communications skills but enrich your life. In terms of communications, knowing more allows you to ask better questions and understand different points of view with less resistance. You can judge situations more effectively and talk about them, whether on the page or in speaking, with greater authority and confidence—all big pluses when you're trying to break through.

CHAPTER FOUR

Do Manners Matter Anymore?

The Strength of Being Gracious and Kind

"WHERE DO YOU THINK YOU'RE GOING?" MY MOTHER SAID from her post at the kitchen sink. I was flying through the house and about to push open the screen door to freedom. To be precise, I was headed to the garage to jump on the new and highly coveted blue banana seat bike my grandparents had given me for my tenth birthday. Stopped in my tracks, I knew the answer to Mom's question was . . . nowhere. I hauled myself back upstairs to my bedroom, where I would stay until I had written a heartfelt thank-you card to my grandparents.

My mom was a drill sergeant about good manners in general and thank-you notes in particular. Marjorie Susman took to parenting with gusto and believed that if she plowed the fields of our young souls with the discipline to be polite and well-mannered, it would yield a bumper crop of children and grandchildren who were respectful, well-behaved, and attentive to the concerns of others. I grumbled over this task at the time, but I was fortunately still a young woman when I recognized its significance and appreciated my mother's diligence in establishing the habit of gratitude in me.

Knowing when to be grateful and how to express it was probably one of the most important lessons I learned from Mom, right up there with where babies come from and how to get designer dresses at discount. Writing thank-you notes became a passion of my own. When I was in my twenties and went to the beach with my friends, I sat under an umbrella with a box of stationery and wrote thank-you notes. "That's weird," my best friend said. I know, but the ritual spoke to me and gave me a sense of connection and pride. What I didn't know until I entered the workforce was that thank-you notes are a powerful professional tool.

When I joined The Estée Lauder Companies in 2000, I found a kindred spirit in my boss, Leonard Lauder. Then chief executive officer of Estée Lauder, Leonard reinforced the profound lessons of gratitude, kindness, and thank-you notes as a communications and managerial tool—not the usual business school fare. I left the company more than a decade ago, but Leonard's words remain with me. "I find that thank-you notes, even a one-liner, help me establish a connection. Once you've established a rapport, you can offer thanks as well as advice and suggestions," he told me.

As of this writing, Leonard remains both chairman emeritus and the family patriarch. He's also a phenomenal communicator. He instilled in me the satisfying practice of regularly expressing generosity through gratitude in the workplace. It's both fulfilling in its own right and a powerful lens through which to express oneself and one's company or cause. In the fall of 2020, Leonard published a wonderful memoir titled *The Company I Keep: My Life in Beauty* about his business and life. My favorite line is, "Nothing makes me happier than writing a good thank-you note." That point of view about the act of putting gratitude in writing is at the core of generosity.

Most everyone in the beauty business knows Leonard as the elegant and thoughtful man who built the empire that carries his mother's name. Estée loved to work with customers personally and expressed her appreciation directly and personally when she saw a customer's face light up after trying a new lip color or scent. This was something Estée Lauder treasured, and she never missed an opportunity to show gracious gratitude to happy customers with a genuine smile and a thank you.

Before he and his mother could afford traditional advertising, they wrote thank-you notes to customers, department store buyers, and the individual saleswomen who worked behind the counters. These memorable handwritten notes made an impact and helped distinguish an upstart brand from the big players in the field. People who received these notes recognized that this cosmetic company was different, more personal. It cared about customers and clients on a deeper level than the bigger players. The personal connection made department store buyers look up and notice the newcomer, and subsequently take a chance on the company's products.

When Leonard took the company public nearly thirty years ago, he sent thank-you notes to everyone who worked on the public offering road show, as well as every potential investor who came to hear his pitch. The November 17, 1995, public offering was a success; by day's end, the stock had increased by 33 percent, thanks to many effective business strategies and the trust and admiration that the Lauder family had built up over decades of expressing gratitude. At the beginning of 2022, The Estée Lauder Companies' market value was around $100 billion.

During the eight years we worked together, Leonard introduced me to many people. I'll never forget the time the two of us stood attentively at a powerful magazine editor's desk as she remained seated, barely making eye contact. Her cool, dismissive demeanor unnerved me, but Leonard remained chipper throughout the brief meeting.

"Don't forget to drop her a thank-you note for seeing us," Leonard said, as we left through the security turnstiles.

"Seriously?" I asked.

"Absolutely," he replied. "That's what we do."

I held my nose while I wrote a thank-you note to that cranky editor. I also realized that Leonard's letter-writing practice is part of the reason why all the editors, even the irascible ones, love him. Showing generosity to rude people undermines their negativity, disarms them, and can often turn their mood or demeanor around.

Leonard's nudge was a crucial lesson, resonating more than all the rest. Simply put, Leonard is generous above all else. He is truly kind. Considerate. He wears his old-world charm on his sleeve. He holds the door for women, listens when others speak, and calls his wife "Darling." Most importantly, he says thank you to everyone, especially those who are too often forgotten or taken for granted—the workers in the manufacturing plant, the security guard in the office lobby, and even a child who showed him a kindness. During my tenure at the company, he sent a thank-you note to my daughter, then six years old, after she left an origami bird she had made on his desk.

Leonard once told me, "Sometimes I write thank-you notes to people for having written me a thank-you note." Over the top? Maybe. Heartfelt? Always. Some may call Leonard old-fashioned. To me, being generous and kind is always in style.

While writing this book, I reached out to Leonard to dig a little deeper into how thank-you notes connect to his business leadership. "Thank-you notes are just so important. People don't work for money alone. They need and deserve praise and gratitude for jobs well done and efforts made. A thank-you note is more than a piece of stationery, it's an acknowledgment that someone has done something well. And that can be so meaningful. Every day, there are people to acknowledge. And I'm not the only one. It's become part of the culture at The Estée Lauder Companies to thank people and to work together with respect and kindness," he explained.

"If you could tell young professionals anything about the art of writing thank-you notes, what would you say?" I asked.

He advised,

> It's more than writing thank-you notes, its acknowledging success and things well done. Do it in a way that is very personal to you and very personal to the person you are writing to. Make sure it doesn't sound canned. Make sure it comes from the heart.
>
> Learn to say thank you. Make it a habit. I understand that when you're stressed out and busy, it may seem like there's no time to say please and thank you. But the more stressed you are, the more important it actually is. Civility and kindness are always key.
>
> When you are applying for a job, it's important to thank all the people who have helped you along in your career. When you're on the job, thank your boss for all that you're learning. Thank your colleagues for teaching you new things. Just as important, when you're leaving a job, do so gracefully. One of the most gracious things you can do is to write a handwritten thank-you note and put it in the mail. You'll be surprised that people remember things like that.
>
> You never know when your paths will cross again, and they likely will. It is strategically wise to leave a pleasant feeling behind as you exit the building.

Leonard's philosophy goes beyond a personal commitment to gratitude. Institutionalized or culture-based consideration is a smart leadership strategy as well. Showing appreciation and recognition to those who deserve it works to engender enthusiasm, hard work, and loyalty. When you look at lists of companies with the lowest turnover rates, "positive environment" is one of the key reasons people stay—right up there with pay and benefits.[1] He helped me understand the importance of gratitude and its place in my daily life. For that, I'm incredibly grateful to him. I think I'll write him a thank-you note.

I keep a gray linen box on my desk that is filled with personalized stationery and funny cards. That makes the ritual of writing thank-you notes easy and enjoyable. Saturday mornings are reserved for reflecting on my week and writing notes. I take comfort in expressing my gratitude to those who covered for me at a crucial meeting, finished a project ahead of deadline, or volunteered for a dreadful duty.

There's a reason why experts list gratitude as an essential ingredient of happiness. Handwriting a note helps me feel connected to loved ones, friends, and colleagues in a world that can sometimes feel divisive and shallow. In the age of email and 280-character proclamations, thank-you notes are more treasured than ever. They are tiny reminders of the limitless potential and power of acting graciously.

There are four truths I've learned about effective thank-you notes, whether an actual handwritten note or an attitude or thank-you mindset.

- *Take time to reflect.* In matters of the heart, speed is rarely a virtue. Before you put pen to paper (or thumbs to text), think about what you want the recipient to know, what sentiment you want to linger, and how you hope they will feel after reading it.

- *Be specific.* The best notes are detailed. Don't just dash off a thank-you note for dinner, but extol the details of the delectable homemade dishes, the beauty of the set table with flowers from the hostess's garden, the delight you took in meeting the fellow guests, mentioning them by name. Go deep. Include something that influenced you. When I sent a note to a former boss thanking her for all that I learned from her, I included the painful feedback she had offered that spurred my professional development.

- *Make it matter.* When any expression of thanks has impact, it has done more than express gratitude—it educates and clarifies, illuminates or incites passion. Offer something of value, an insight, or a piece of information. Recently, I sent thank-you notes to my neighbors for their thoughtfulness during the Covid lockdown, noting how their sense of community during a hard time helped me feel safe and supported.

- *It's never too late.* Even if the gift came six months ago or longer, it's better to write the note than not. Apologize for being tardy, move on without further excuse, and express your feelings. The recipient will appreciate it and forgive your lateness on the spot. It can take years to fully realize the impact of a person on your life. Don't let this stop you from expressing your gratitude. I ask you to consider if there is anyone to whom you owe a thank-you letter.

Thanking Big

During the time I was communicating Pfizer's response to the pandemic, I knew I was in the company of a great team of professionals. Even so, I admit to being amazed and quite humbled by the dedication our teams, in every department and level of the company, showed in doing their part to find a way out of the virus that had changed our lives forever. As I worked on in-house and outward-facing information, I heard Leonard whisper in my mind's ear. *Why don't you write a thank-you note?* Yes! Pfizer scientists, our manufacturing colleagues, administrative personnel, clinical trial volunteers—all of them had gone above and beyond the loftiest expectations. If I was going to extend thanks, it had to be done publicly and in a way that pointed out the hard work of many at a time when the need was so great.

In the months that followed, we wrote thank-you notes in the form of full-page banner advertisements, each under one of our values: courage, excellence, and joy. The first one was headlined "Courage," and it came in conjunction with submission of our Covid-19 vaccine for emergency-use authorization to the US FDA. The ad was directed to the more than 46,000 brave clinical trial volunteers who rolled up their sleeves and took a shot before we knew if the vaccine was effective. They of all people deserve credit for *their* selfless act of generosity. The second ad was titled "Joy" and ran in the *New York Times*, *Washington Post*, and other national and local outlets on December 15, 2020, following the FDA's emergency-use authorization for our Covid-19 vaccine four days prior. This one applauded the scientists who "hung on when long hours turned into late nights, when defeat seemed inevitable, they pushed through. When the theories crumbled, the strategies collapsed, and the pressure began to mount . . ."

The third one, titled "Excellence" was directed to our frontline manufacturing colleagues. This followed a visit by President Biden to our plant in Kalamazoo, Michigan, and a tour by European Commissioner Thierry Breton to our factory in Puurs, Belgium. We wanted to show our appreciation to the women and men who worked through the pandemic, producing vaccines in record time and number. This ad acknowledged "a team willing to prioritize the greater good." We spent our advertising dollars not for marketing, but for *mattering*. We said that which was most important to say.

These communications were highly effective, demonstrated in part by the numerous overwhelmingly positive responses we received from colleagues and stakeholders. Our brand awareness increased by 66 percent in 2020. This advertising series demonstrated Pfizer's humanity and humility by acknowledging the many people around us, inside and outside our company, who made our success possible and those we continued to wish to serve. The effort came across as sincere because it was, and I believe most who saw it felt that way too. Companies, especially, must make the time to show gratitude to all those who contributed to their successes not as a marketing ploy but as a genuine acknowledgment that no one gets any place good on their own.

You're Welcome . . . Have a Seat

The art of acting out of graciousness has been popularized and per-fected by my friend, rock star restaurateur, and communicator ex-traordinaire, Danny Meyer. Not only is he a brave communicator, as I discussed in chapter 2, he's a generous and kind one. In Danny's commitment to what he calls "enlightened hospitality," no detail is too small. Its basic tenets form a genius and effective business plan and a brilliant, nuanced communications strategy. I'm fortunate to have deepened my friendship with Danny in recent years. We are neighbors in Manhattan, and in full disclosure, I'm a regular at Union Square Cafe (table 44). I've had the chance to see this intimate, high-impact hospitality up close. On our first return visit to Union Square Cafe after the pandemic, I was greeted with a note from the team wel-coming me back, saying they missed me and thanking me for trusting them to return to indoor dining post pandemic.

Danny's method connects people and creates community. First, he carefully considers language. For example, Danny instructs his staff to never say, "How was everything?" as guests depart because it's a trans-actional comment usually met with a "fine." Rather, the team will say, "It was so lovely to have you with us this evening" or "We look for-ward to welcoming you again soon," which is warmer and assumes a relationship.

When Danny makes an argument or debates a point, with his em-ployees or his guests, his neighbors or competitors, he uses his en-lightened hospitality business practice that "nothing is as important as how one is made to feel." In his view, they should feel included in the conversation, and they should be respected when he makes his own point of view known. I asked Danny whether my assessment was right. In true Danny form, he demurred, deflected my admiration, and quoted Maya Angelou as saying, "I've learned that people will forget what you said, people will forget what you did, but people will never forget how you made them feel."

I was impressed when, after the draining 2020 election was called, Danny tweeted, "To friends who feel deflated tonight: a virtual hug. To those who feel elated: enjoy this uplifting moment. Time for all of us to show the virtue of leading with hospitality. Much hard work to do, many big problems to solve. Nothing possible without a place at the table for all." Such rare civility! He wasn't canceling people for not agreeing with him; he was asking everyone to come together. This is a vital reminder to extend the hand of fellowship and reach across the social and political divides. We cannot communicate effectively if we dismiss people and refuse to listen or speak to them. It's very bad for business, but mainly, it's dangerous for civil society. Someday we may find ourselves being canceled.

Let's Cancel the Cancel Culture

What response is the least gracious, most ungenerous, and completely unkind? It's the brutal smackdown of cancel culture. It's a slap that scars and shuts down any avenue for mutual understanding and dialogue.

Cancel culture, also known as callout culture, came into the collective consciousness around 2015, as a phrase first used by hip-hop artists who felt sidelined by those who deemed their actions or words unacceptable.[2] It's nothing new, however. Public shaming and shunning have been around since biblical times, when John the Baptist, the itinerant Jewish preacher, was beheaded by Herod for saying the wrong things. It hit its stride in the Middle Ages when citizens and monks alike were cast out of communities for breaking vows or holding unpopular views.[3] It has long been fodder for fairy tales, parables, and novels. Nathaniel Hawthorne's classic *The Scarlet Letter* shows Hester Prynne and her daughter as victims of the American Puritan version of cancel culture, not as an endorsement of it, but as a warning.

Today, cancel culture spreads like a rapidly moving virus thanks to social media. Its latest iteration involves politicians on both sides of the aisle who use it to decry and ostracize anyone with a dissenting view or unconventional behavior of any kind. Cancel culture is ubiquitous in business, the arts, education, and almost every corner of society. It's easy to ferret out something "unacceptable" to pin on someone, because social media posts and commentary never die. Journalist and entrepreneur Arianna Huffington calls it the "eternal archive."[4]

When cancel culture fever rises, no one is safe. Not even the iconic figurine Mr. Potato Head, who in 2021 was rendered "genderless" by its producer, the multinational toy company Hasbro. Not Dr. Seuss, when the custodians of Theodor Geisel's estate, Dr. Seuss Enterprises, consulted with a "panel of experts" and decided to cease publishing six Seuss titles because they "portray people in ways that are hurtful and wrong."[5]

Not even my beloved Laura Ingalls Wilder is safe. I nearly drove my car into a ditch when I heard NPR radio report in June of 2018 that the American Library Association had voted unanimously to strip Laura Ingalls Wilder's name from a major children's literature award over concerns for how the author referred to Indigenous and Black people. As referenced in the previous chapter on curiosity, the *Little House* book series based on Wilder's life transported me as a girl. In hindsight, her references are antiquated and stereotypical, but they represent the mindset and language of her time.

Cancel culture zealots scare me in the same way that bullies do. They pile on. Capitalize on a moment of perceived weakness. The fist shakers know to attack a vulnerable politician ahead of an election or to pounce on a weak business leader during a time of employee unrest. They leave no room for reconciliation. Knowing no one is immune, it's hard to argue against keeping one's trap shut. I'm not always as brave as I'd like to be in the face of cancel culture's angry mob. But I commit to being more courageous and advocating for fair hearings, open discussion, and the hard work of reconciliation. I hope you'll join me.

I realize I'm writing on thin ice here because too many people have become overly rigid about what they consider to be right and wrong in terms of acceptable political and cultural opinions. I get it. Surely, there are ways to update and educate without stripping and denouncing. Shouldn't we discuss the bias that existed in the past and the pain it caused without pulling books from the shelves? Isn't there a teachable moment here? Why not publish an addendum or convene a conversation? I believe we, as a society, are capable of more than briskly eliminating that which appalls us or even simply annoys us. I want to live in a world that has the capacity for kindness, redemption, *and* forgiveness.

I'm Jewish, but I was raised in a family that celebrated Jewish and non-Jewish holidays alike. My two favorites are Thanksgiving and Yom Kippur. I was born on November 24, 1961, the day after Thanksgiving. My birth stories include hearing how my mom enjoyed her turkey and stuffing and then headed to the hospital's maternity ward. On many years, my birthday falls on Thanksgiving or during the long holiday weekend. So, I feel a connection via the calendar but also for the rituals of the celebratory feast that brings family and friends together in a grateful spirit. My second most cherished day is Yom Kippur, the day of atonement. It is, for me, the quietest day of the year. I don't belong to a temple, and I often fail in my halfhearted attempt at fasting, but I do make sure to find time for true reflection and atonement. This year I found a bench in a nearby park where I sat and recalled my mistakes, people I've inadvertently hurt, or promises I've not fulfilled. Wherever possible I try to make amends.

How can we grow as a society if we do not allow people to evolve through education and forgiveness? That goes for us as well—we might be wrong, too.

In terms of breakthrough communications, it means using all the tools in this book to address those opinions with which we disagree or find troublesome. Use grace and kindness to understand another point of view; sometimes the truth *is* found in the other, but we won't know that until we listen and try to understand.

Practices of Gracious and Kind Communicators

You can have a profound and positive effect on people with gracious communication. What follows are key concepts of kindness and graciousness essential for breaking through.

First, graciousness breaks down defensiveness. No matter how hostile the interrogator, whether an angry congressman at a public hearing or an aggressive moderator of an unwelcoming panel, I always begin my first response with, "Thank you so much for inviting me here today." Even if I'd rather be having a root canal, I offer my gratitude for being included. It both lightens the mood and opens the ears.

Second, generous communicators give credit where credit is due. People like to be told they are doing a good job, and even more, they appreciate it when their special efforts are highlighted. Research shows many employees say it is "extremely important" to be recognized by their managers—but do you really need a study to tell you that?[6] I don't think so. I know it from my own experience as an employee. In almost every case, the reason I left a job was because I felt my supervisor, or my company, no longer appreciated me. And, in all candor, I've lost some of my most talented team members because I failed to convey directly and clearly how much they mattered to me and to the mission we were pursuing.

Third, kind communicators allow the other person space. Don't catch people off guard or off their game when approaching them to have an important conversation. It's not fair, and not smart. Just because you've knocked on someone's door and they've answered doesn't mean it's the best time to have a deep conversation with them. Ask a colleague or customer if they are available to discuss what's on your mind and if not, ask when *do* they have the time. I begin almost every phone call with, "Do you have a moment?" or "Is this a good time?"

Fourth, clarity wins, ambiguity loses. Not being clear is thoughtless and unproductive. It can be seen as manipulative. One of my favorite rules of speech-making has three steps: (1) tell them what you are going to say, (2) say it, and (3) then tell them what you said. It's the kind way to organize your remarks and makes listening easier.

Gracious communicators share their agenda. Lay it out. Why are people in a meeting with you? Tell them. What do you want subordinates or teammates to accomplish? Let them know. What is expected of the people who work for you? What do customers or constituents need to know about what you're up to? Good intentions are great, but only if you are generous enough to share them. Don't be stingy with important information. It's not a power play to keep people guessing. If you want to get the best out of everyone, be clear with setting expectations.

Fifth, generous communicators know the difference between "I" and "we" and use them appropriately. This is especially true when it comes to taking blame and assigning it correctly when things go wrong. Dallas Mavericks owner Mark Cuban once commented about a star player's missed game-tying free-throw shot. He said, "He made the first shot, and *we* missed the second."[7] These subtle uses of "he" and "we" was inherently generous. Cuban gave the player credit for making the first shot but did not blame him for missing the second. In the process he reminded observers that sports depend on teamwork to succeed, and players are in it together. They give credit when a player exceeds expectations, but we all take the fall together.

When my boss Albert Bourla was invited to write a piece for *Harvard Business Review* (HBR) early in 2021, the editors told us the column would be focused on the incredible accomplishments under pressure and titled "How I Did It."[8] We told them we'd love to provide the column, but it had to be under the framing of "How We Did It."

HBR accepted the change and said that would be the model going forward. I'm proud of that, as it exemplifies the posture of generosity we want to convey in our communications.

Next, kind communicators know what *not* to say. Just because you can say something doesn't mean you should say it. Recently, I was on a panel discussing the vaccine, and one of my panel mates took credit for something that had actually happened at Pfizer. The hair on the back of my neck went up. My first impulse was to attack him for taking credit for our work. But I took a deep breath and thought better of it and let it go. Decide before you correct something, point out a flaw, or offer a criticism, whether it's worth it or not. What end are you seeking? If it's not to actually help someone but to aggrandize yourself, it's best to keep quiet.

Avoid alienating details and insider jargon that leave the average listener on the sidelines. Using technical language doesn't make you sound smart. You sound arrogant. I particularly detest elitist language: Did we need to know that your car was a Ferrari? Please let's avoid the humble brag on your Instagram: "So grateful to Harvard for offering my son a full scholarship!" Many emotions are more powerfully expressed in private.

Don't go overboard. Be careful not to tip over into being obsequious. Nobody likes that kind of unctuous behavior that makes one appear to be fawning. I don't.

Finally (don't follow my example here), generous communicators don't save the best for last. Begin any communication with what's important. Share good news first. Praise should always precede criticism, and conversations, especially tough ones, should end on a positive note.

One of my favorite world-class communicators is the late Mr. Rogers, the public television children's show host who reached thousands of American kids each afternoon, offering them comfort and connection in his famous neighborhood. Fred Rogers was a brave and big-hearted communicator who tackled difficult subjects ranging from physical disability to isolation and loneliness. He knew the importance of ending each show in an upbeat way. His concluding comments were always, "You've made this day a special day, by just your being you. There's no person in the whole world like you, and I like you just the way you are." Mr. Rogers, like all sensitive communicators, was careful to leave the listeners better than he found them.

And speaking of listeners, when you are on the receiving end, be mindful to be gracious too. When I'm in the audience, if the speaker catches my eye, I give a quick nod to signal that I'm receiving. I acknowledge emails, even if it's just with a "Got it." Every thank-you deserves a heartfelt, "You're welcome." As a communicator, I try to live in the language of kindness. It's more than polite. It's powerful.

CHAPTER FIVE

Measure Up to the Moment

Take Time to Pause and Prepare

ALMOST EVERY BIG MISTAKE I MAKE IS THE RESULT OF rushing. When I dive headlong into action without stopping for reflection or jump to conclusions without reading the signposts along the way, disaster looms. That was surely the case on August 8, 2003, when I leaped before I looked and wound up embarrassing myself on the front page of the *Wall Street Journal*.

The day before publication, the phone rang in my office. When I answered, two *Wall Street Journal* reporters, Kate Kelly and Shelly Branch, were on the line, asking for an interview. That was unusual. As Estée Lauder Companies' chief communicator, normally I'd be dialing their numbers and doing the outreach—and the pitch. That turnabout in roles should have been my first clue. The reporters mumbled something about an article on fashionable female executives. That kind of girlie journalism was the lifeblood of the beauty business. We relied on editors' interest in the fashion predilections and beauty secrets of our high-profile women, including celebrity spokesmodel Elizabeth Hurley or our company founder Estée Lauder's glamorous granddaughter Aerin Lauder. My job was to broker those requests and negotiate the details.

To my surprise, these journalists were interested in me. "*Me?*" I remember saying.

"Yes," they chimed in unison. "We've heard wonderful things about you. Will you tell us about a presentation you gave recently?" one asked. At that moment, my brain must have shut off. "Sure!" I replied.

I began to natter with the duo then and there without doing even a shred of the most basic due diligence for myself that I would have conducted for any executive I was supporting. I would have made sure to understand the story angle and ask who else was being interviewed, what deadlines they were facing, and how facts would be checked, and quotes verified. That morning, I didn't ask enough questions. Heck, I don't think I asked any questions at all. My ego had been disarmed, and it had shifted me into a forward-moving gear without doing any of these routine checks.

The reporters warmed me up with some softballs: "How long have you had such an amazing job? Tell us about your career path? What do you like to wear to work?" I was so wrapped up in the stories of my successes and beguiled by my own charm that I failed to see the trap.

"We heard a funny story from a recent speech you gave. Tell us about it," one reporter said. At this point I was rolling. My mouth was running on autopilot. I desperately wanted to amuse and delight these two women on the other end of the phone.

So, I indulged them—and myself—by telling the story of how I was stricken by a toe cramp while presenting on a main stage, thanks to the torture of my trendy pointy-toed shoes. The minute it was out of my mouth, I realized the mistake. Like a polar bear breaking through the ice and hurtling into the freezing waters, by the time I knew what was happening, it was too late.

"Thanks!" the reporters said in unison and hung up the phone before I had the chance to try to reel my words back. Even before the story ran, I knew I'd made an unforced error. Two lessons I already knew were going to be reinforced the hard way: you're never too experienced to make a mistake, and you're rarely self-aware enough not to be seduced by flattery.

I tell you this story not because of any real interest in pointy shoes or a fashion faux pas but because leaders and communicators need to have the patience and discipline to pause and prepare to avoid calamity. My instinct to please, to answer every question asked, is not smart. The ability to wait and line up your thoughts, arguments, support materials, rebuttal, and conclusions is the mark of a wise spokesperson.

The next morning, my name appeared on the front page under the headline, "Agony of the Feet: Fashion Says If the Shoe Fits, What's the Point?"[1] It was the A-hed. For the uninitiated in journalism lingo, A-hed is the most prominent position in the center and the top of the front page. And just beneath the headline, there was the byline of those two rascals, Kate Kelly and Shelly Branch. I felt as if I could see them smirking at me.

Then in the lede, the article's opening paragraph: "Standing tall and chic in a pair of pointy-toed pumps, Sally Susman confidently conducted a presentation to a group of Estée Lauder executives. Then the unspeakable happened. 'This pain shot up my leg. It hurt so bad that I thought I would pass out,' says Ms. Susman, an Estée Lauder senior vice president, who managed to steel her way through the speech before limping off to free her toes and groan."[2]

The article then regaled readers with anecdotes on the latest toe tonics, blister bandages, and even the uptick in toe-shortening surgery. I was humiliated. My cheeks flushed as I read the story. There it was in print. The most reputable and serious business newspaper had featured me not for a winning communications strategy or a brilliant marketing campaign, but for a toe cramp. Ouch. I slunk into my office that morning, sat frozen at my desk, and read the piece one more time. Then, I buried my copy into the waste bin and hoped that, somehow, everyone would miss the story. Or at least be kind enough to let it pass without mention.

In fact, *no one* said a word to me about it. Not a single peep. As I walked through the corridors that day, most of my colleagues just averted their eyes. Executives kept their doors closed. Administrative assistants became engrossed in their typing. I imagined they were thinking that I was a lousy media relations expert, that I couldn't even handle my own press. I was like a barefoot cobbler. I hung my head most of the day.

Just before quitting time, my assistant popped into my office and said, "Mr. Lauder's on your line." As noted earlier, that would be Leonard Lauder, the company CEO, and my boss. My heart began to pump, and my throat snapped dry. Would he harangue me over this faux pas? Might he fire me? I closed my eyes, picked up the receiver, and prepared to take my beating.

"Well, they said you were tall and chic," Leonard said. "How wonderful!" His charitable interpretation and kindness once again amazed me. I'm not sure what I said next. It was a short conversation. My hands were still trembling when I returned the receiver to its cradle. I pulled the article from the bottom of my office trash can and reread it with a less critical eye. Leonard's gracious comment restored my self-esteem.

In that moment I was reminded of a few basic, but important media relations rules:

- *Understand what is at stake.* You are allowed to question reporters. When a reporter asks for an interview, be sure you ask up front about the story's angle and the writer's perspective on it. Even friendly reporters are doing a job, and they don't work for you.

- *Weigh the risk and reward of participating in the piece.*
  Contrary to the opinion of some, not all press is good press.
  You are allowed to say "no comment" or decline an interview
  request. You do not have to answer a reporter's questions.

- *Mistakes and misstatements happen.* Own them, but don't let
  an errant comment derail you. Don't take everything personally. Never let your skin become too thin for the rough and
  tumble of the work. Give the boss a heads-up if the news is
  negative or when you may be part of a story. Alert your boss to
  what she may read in the papers the next day. Manage the situation. Communication surprises are always a bad thing in the
  corporate world, even if the resulting story is positive. People in
  large and small organizations like to know who their people are
  talking to and why.

I made several promises to myself that day. I would do the ground-
work necessary before accepting any more personal interview requests (should any reporter ever want to talk to me again). If I screwed
up in the future, I'd chuckle along with the joke. Laughing at yourself
makes you look beautiful. I realized resilience was more relevant than
fashion. My toe cramp had morphed into a turning point. And for the
record, I no longer wear pointy shoes. Never. I've forsaken the torture of narrow-toed and spindly high heels for comfortable and lovely
round-toed chunky-heeled models. Safely ensconced in them, I'm
strong and steady. They ground me. My toes are happier and so am I.

Believe in the Pause

Today I'm committed to slowing down and reminding myself that
only fools rush in. Apparently, I'm not the only one who has made
an unforced error caused by thoughtless speed. We see this mistake
through human history. Over four hundred years ago, in William

Shakespeare's immortal play *Romeo and Juliet*, Friar Laurence warns Romeo against recklessness, which ultimately proves fatal for the young lovers. He tells them to go "wisely and slow, they stumble that run fast."

If you watch closely, almost every professional of any stripe will take a pause before the moment of truth. Pro golfers take a deep breath before they tee off. Concert pianists wait a beat and settle themselves before striking the keys.

I try, but it's not easy to slow my roll. Once I went on a silent retreat at the Garrison Institute in upstate New York in search of answers to midcareer questions. Rather than finding quiet contemplation, I nearly lost my mind, so ill-equipped was I for calm and quietude. As you may recall in the first chapter, during my yoga practice intended to "clear my mind," my brain was filled with thoughts of work. Sometimes I struggle to meditate even for a few minutes. Whenever I try to follow the yogi's instruction to slow, deepen, and watch my breathing, I involuntarily hyperventilate. Can't seem to help it. I feel as though I may suffocate. But I persist in the pursuit of a meaningful pause because I believe it's essential for one's health *and* as an effective communications tool.[3]

Breakthrough communicators use the silence of a pause strategically. In speeches, silence is a powerful way to underscore a point just made. Take a moment to let the thought sink in with your audience. Let the quiet reflect the certainty you have in the worthiness of your opinion. In more than one speech that I've drafted for an executive, I have injected humor. When I do, I insert the marker [pause for laughter] to remind the speaker to take a beat, let the audience hear and process the joke, and show confidence that the laughter will flow. Some anxious presenters will plow on and crush the moment.

Shifting perspective, beware of reporters' use of silence. I've heard many journalists ask a question and then, after it's answered, the reporter waits. What follows is a long, pregnant pause. It's a game of chicken. Who can sit more comfortably in the silence? Even experienced people can find these silences disconcerting and awkward and fill the gap by prattling on, often giving away more information than they intended. A study by Harvard psychology researcher Adam M. Mastroianni found that most people don't know how to end a conversation and have trouble finding a good place to stop.[4] Two things happen in conversations, especially with a stranger, in this case, a reporter. The two parties don't know what each other wants, and the two parties want different things from the conversation. Silence in the other party can encourage someone to keep going, and reporters don't need a Harvard study to tell them that it works to get a subject to keep revealing themselves. Hold out. Stare back. Sit on your hands. Think about errands you have to run. Anything to keep you from continuing to yack past the answer you were asked to provide.

Avoid being a blurter. I learned this lesson early in my career—otherwise known as "discretion is the better part of valor" (an expression that holds profound truth). In my first job, when I was working for Senator Thomas Eagleton, I learned that he was planning to retire. This information was not to be made public; it was a personal decision that Senator Eagleton had a right to announce on his own timeline. But the information was burning within me. I was young and trying to impress people with my knowledge and (nonexistent) power. I told a friend, who, in what became a humiliating game of telephone, passed along the information. Ultimately the story broke in the media, and the finger pointed to me as the weak link in the chain of confidentiality.

My shame and the impact of my indiscretion hung in the air of the Senate office like a bad odor. If I had only paused to think, to calm the nervous energy that having a piece of proprietary information gives you, I would have known better than to open my mouth. I lost a great deal of credibility, and while Senator Eagleton forgave me, our relationship was never the same and I never enjoyed the same level of trust.

So, remember that in speeches, interviews, and in any important exchange, you don't have to fill the void with chatter. A pause is not a period. It's a comma. A breath. A moment filled with so much opportunity to make the next right decision.

Be ready with some safe harbors. Even savvy former White House press secretary Jen Psaki was known to say she would have to "circle back on that one." Of course, she did. No one knows the answer to every question. It's a ridiculous expectation. The job is to answer what you know and find out what you don't. And you must be religious about truly returning to the questioner with an answer in real time. My favorite safe harbor is to say, "That's a really interesting question. Let me reflect on it and get back to you." At that point, I gather all my composure and stare straight back at my interrogator, saying not another word. Not one word. It takes practice and control—both learnable.

Prepare for Questions

Beyond a healthy respect for the pause, it's crucial for every leader to prepare for each engagement. I've seen highly skilled communicators crash when overconfidence takes hold, and they don't see the need to ready themselves. As Benjamin Franklin said, "By failing to prepare, you are preparing to fail." So, yes, something as seemingly basic as preparation is every bit as crucial as channeling your intention, mustering your courage for candor, or any of the other principles in this book, even for the most experienced leaders. But how to prepare?

First, build your own methodology. There's no singular system that's universally accepted as the optimal one for communicators. For this book, I first spent a lot of time up front on the outline, which provided a road map of the sections that would be researched and written, and the direction those sections would take. I cannot overstate the importance of creating the structure and outline in any written or oral communiqué. Next, I gathered my thoughts in the way I was taught to prep for debate club in seventh grade. I jotted down every idea on a lined, three-by-five index card and then organized the cards into a box with yellow stickies dividing sections. It's not high-tech, but it works for me. Find the techniques that deliver for you.

Second, sign up for training. Never feel embarrassed to ask for help. Most heads of state and chief executives, even those who are at the top of their game, undergo speech delivery and media training before, or in expectation of, high-profile engagements that come with those jobs. In 2010, arguably the best tech journalist in the business and founder of Recode, Kara Swisher, and her equally forceful colleague *Wall Street Journal* tech reporter Walt Mossberg sat down with Facebook CEO Mark Zuckerberg, for a high-pressure interview centering on problems around privacy abuses on the social media platform.[5]

After just a few minutes of tough questions, Zuckerberg started to perspire visibly, so much so, he had to remove his trademark hoodie. The interview did not go well for him. It didn't matter what he said at that point; everyone then and now focused on the sweat pouring down his face and soaking his gray T-shirt. Eight years later, in preparing for a grilling before Congress, Zuckerberg went through intense media coaching.[6] The interview went better, although Facebook and its founder continue to face tough questions and continue to trip up on some of the answers—a topic for another book.

I like to bring in a consultant or trusted confidant, who, by virtue of their independence, is often more able to speak the blunt truths that leaders need to hear but often don't from the people around them. An outsider who is being paid to tell the truth doesn't face the same pressures as a staff member does in the sticky situation of having to tell your fearless leader that they lack charm or composure.

I had the tremendous opportunity to be trained by Anita Dunn when she was at her public relations firm SKDKnickerbocker. (As I write, Anita is a senior adviser to President Biden and leading communications strategy in the White House.) Anita played, very convincingly, the role of a tough interviewer, peppered me with questions, and taped the exchange on video. I saw I had a nervous tic of nodding compulsively. Even when the questioner was attacking me, my head was bobbing up and down as if in agreement. The overall effect was that I looked anxious. I hadn't noticed this previously and no one on my team had told me. I was so grateful to Anita for having the courage to point that out, and I've learned how to hold myself steady and appear calm and in command during TV interviews, even when I'm not.

Journalist and television personality Jonathan Capehart (who we will meet again later in this book) spent time earlier in his career providing media training. "For most people, talking to the press is like talking to the cops. They are a little afraid. I explain that the power of the journalists ends the moment they finish asking the question. That's when you have the power to answer or not answer, figure a way to pivot, bridge to a better topic. Now that I'm back in journalism, my ears are tuned to these techniques, and I understand what my interviewee is doing. I admire those who do it well and they make for some of the best guests on my show and most interesting conversations," Jonathan said. I try to remember this wisdom and take the power back when it's my turn to speak.

Third, take care not to overprepare. A former colleague of mine, who had the office next door, used to read his remarks aloud over and over to commit them to memory. I felt sorry for the guy every time I heard his rehearsal through our shared wall. In his attempt to remember every word, he often appeared too studied and nervous, and his presentation felt forced.

Rather than my office neighbor's cramming-for-the-test technique, my recommendation is to truly pause. Before you stroll onto the stage for a speech or see the camera light blink on for a TV interview, try to step back from your notes. Breathe. Remember, you were invited to this forum because you are an expert. Own your story and speak from the heart. You may not be word perfect, but chances are you will be engaging and surely know more than most in your audience. I hate to see interviews or speeches fall flat when the answers people give are canned, or the presenter looks overly rehearsed. Never memorize!

Find a Framework

As leaders, it's our job to prepare for the storms headed our direction. But it's hard to see around every corner and impossible to anticipate every eventuality. In fact, you cannot. There's no way to have a briefing document, contingency memo, or talking points to anticipate every scenario. I realized that when I found myself awash in issues following the 2016 US presidential election. With President Trump's victory, there was a rash of questions that came in my direction. Would our company support the Women's March in Washington the day after the inauguration? Did we have a position on the so-called war on science? What was our stance on whether undocumented people should be allowed to use our social services? Did we think the United States should remain in the Paris Climate Agreement? My head was spinning.

This time I paused. Rather than run each issue up the corporate flagpole and debate the pros and cons, I chose to create a framework by which we could make the decision to opine, or not, on breaking issues based on agreed-on metrics. Why not? All other big corporate choices had an agreed-on set of measures and hurdles by which to run the company: when to invest, how to appraise productivity, how to calculate risk. But on the question of when and how to wade into public affairs waters, we were far less clear. This was my area of expertise, and I was chagrined that my domain lacked the discipline and rigor the others (finance, manufacturing, legal, etc.) had refined.

My fellow executive committee members offered to help me write the formula. We gathered in the company board room and started brainstorming. Candidly, it was hard for me to listen to my colleagues' views, some of whom had no particular expertise in my area. Some were scientists, others were lawyers, a few were accountants. I consciously worked not to be defensive. And, because I sat back and listened, I heard several good suggestions from people I may have wrongly dismissed had I created a wall between them and me. These are smart, experienced leaders, and I suspected my framework would be stronger for their input. So, I once again parked my ego and started taking notes on a large easel. Old fashioned, I know, but effective.

Our framework has five questions:

1. *Does the issue relate to our purpose?* This question is a meaningful brake to prevent a company from weighing in on every issue. It is not necessary to offer a viewpoint on every single cultural whim or social movement—in many cases, silence is golden. Most consumers don't think about where Pfizer or any other company stands on every issue facing society. They want to know where we stand on issues related to what we do. In large companies, there will be an advocate (or a critic) on every public controversy, but individual interest shouldn't govern. And not all issues are equal. Speaking out on too many topics erodes one's agency. Don't overuse your microphone or people will stop listening. Focus your advocacy on issues that resonate with your purpose.

2. *How does the matter impact our stakeholders?* This question must be thoughtfully answered, especially in cases where stakeholders' interests may be in conflict. There are so many topics, from climate change to parental leave, where arguments for and against can quickly combust with different constituencies on either side. For me, there is one constituency above all others: an institution's employees. Their views take priority. Staff who feel ignored or alienated are often your most troublesome detractors. By contrast, those employees who feel heard and understood are your greatest ambassadors.

3. *What are our choices for engagement?* You always have options in terms of response modes and actions, though they may not be obvious in the moment. Do not become a prisoner of other people's agendas and plans when pressured to "sign our petition" or "add your CEO's name to our open letter" or "Get back to me before my deadline today!" Design and follow your own

thought-out strategies. Choose the message and messenger that most clearly expresses your view. Following our experience with Albert's colleague letter that went viral after the Trump-Biden presidential debate, my preferred way to get on the record for a hot topic is to have the boss send an internal message that we then make public. It's controlled and executed on our own terms.

4. *What is the price of our silence?* This question often trumps the others. An issue may not be precisely on point to our purpose, the views of stakeholders may not be obvious, but the cost of saying nothing is just too great. Silence on some topics—such as racism, homophobia, anti-Semitism, and other matters of humanity—is unacceptable. For example, after white suprem-acists rallied in Charlottesville, Virginia, in August of 2017, many companies spoke out. At Pfizer we issued an all-colleague note from our CEO that began, "Dear Colleagues, I'm writing regarding the bigotry and violence we saw in Charlottesville, Virginia, this past weekend. The racism that was on dis-play has no place in a civilized world. The hate groups—and individuals—behind this weekend's vitriol and violence are not welcome in our communities and need to be held accountable for their actions." Two years later, in 2019, the Business Round-table (BRT) redefined the purpose of corporations, moving away from shareholder primacy, and including comments to all stakeholders. Pfizer signed alongside 180 other major multina-tional companies. This declaration set a new bar for leadership that included more robust public engagement.

5. *How does the issue relate to our values?* This question was provoked by our BRT statement. An additional layer of con-sideration is an important one. Our Pfizer values are courage, excellence, equity, and joy. Any of these can stir us to action.

This framework makes my job easier and more efficient. Using a scaffolding allows us to hit the ground running in terms of the actual work to be done. I may not know what tomorrow's controversy will be, but I do know how I'll evaluate it for my company. Here I'm aligned with the decorated war general and US president Dwight D. Eisenhower who said, "Plans are worthless, but planning is everything." I encourage you to find a framework that best suits you (or feel free to use ours) or claim whatever structure allows you to always feel ready to face anything that comes your way.

When Crisis Comes: A Checklist

When a crisis hits, and it's a safe bet that it will, a wrong response can trash in a moment the strong public image built and cultivated over years, hence, the phrase that reputation is earned in drops and lost in buckets. These reputation spills seem guaranteed to keep flowing.

In February of 2022, Spotify's chief executive Daniel Ek had to apologize to employees for the way mega-podcaster Joe Rogan used racial slurs. Ek wrote in a letter to employees, "There are no words I can say to adequately convey how deeply sorry I am for the way 'The Joe Rogan Experience' controversy continues to impact you. Not only are some of Joe Rogan's comments incredibly hurtful, but I also want to make clear that they do not represent the values of this company." I admire the way Ek moved quickly to clarify his views with his most important constituency—Spotify's employees.

One month later, the behemoth Disney Corporation was in a public relations crossfire when the company had originally declined to take a stand on proposed legislation in Florida that restricted classroom discussion of gender identity and sexual orientation. When Disney employees revolted over the company's silence, the CEO responded with an about-face and opposed the bill. The Florida governor fired back by revoking a 1967 law that allowed Walt Disney to function as its own quasi-government. Heads were spinning, and Geoff Morrell, who Disney hired only two months earlier as chief corporate affairs officer, was out of a job.

Some infamous incidents are so profound they lodge themselves in our collective psyche. Can anyone forget:

- President Bill Clinton wagging his finger in the final moments of an address from the White House in January 1998 saying he "did not have sexual relations with that woman, Ms. Lewinsky." By August of that same year, President Clinton admitted in grand jury testimony that he had engaged in an "improper physical relationship" with the twenty-two-year-old intern, Monica Lewinsky. Further investigations led to charges of perjury and impeachment by the House of Representatives. In addition to the moral failure, the president's lie was a highly visible communications debacle that deepened the country's animosity toward him.

- Wells Fargo, the second largest bank in the United States, digging itself into a deep hole when, in 2016, authorities were alerted to potential fraud after some employees at local branches responded to an aggressive top-down demand for customer quotas by creating nearly 2 million fake bank accounts in customers' names but without their consent. After the scandal was made public, Wells Fargo leaders' public statements did not accept responsibility, nor did they apologize. Instead, company executives downplayed the fraud. The CEO only uttered "I'm sorry" when he testified before the US Senate Banking Committee. Instead, the leaders blamed and fired 5,300 low-level rank-and-file employees. The CEO also sold $61 million of his Wells Fargo stock the month before the investigation began.[7]

- The video feed of crude oil pouring into the Gulf of Mexico following the explosion of the Deepwater Horizon oil rig operated by British Petroleum (BP) on April 20, 2010. Eleven people died and 134 million gallons of oil polluted the gulf in an environmental catastrophe and public relations debacle. Bad enough, but the communications gaffe that did even more to damage the company's reputation was when then–BP CEO Tony Hayward complained to reporters that he wanted "his life back," as if responding to the disaster was an annoying personal inconvenience.[8]

These fiascos are forever etched in my mind and remain cautionary tales. Communications gaffes resulted in a popular president, a historic financial institution, and an established multinational corporation bearing negative marks on their legacies. Could a wise adviser have made a difference? Not always, but in many cases, I believe, the answer is yes.

Crises take different shapes. Some are accidents and others devious plots. Some erupt in a flash, while others slowly boil over years. All involve a grave loss of some sort—of dignity, or security, or one of many other precious qualities, most importantly, trust. While you can never know what precise circumstances you might face in any given crisis, you can prepare by understanding certain basics.

Gather facts quickly and methodically. Knowing how to ask the most relevant questions is crucial in a communications crisis. At my first public relations job at American Express in 1990, I watched my boss, Senior Vice President for Communications Mike O'Neill, respond to a variety of breakdowns ranging from a feared data breach of card member accounts to merchant revolts due to Amex's high fees, by calmly sitting at his desk and ticking through his list of questions. Naive and new to the field, I remember thinking, what's wrong with this guy? Why is he just sitting there asking all these questions? He should start telling us what to do.

Mike's method of meticulous questioning is essential to crisis communications management. Often a communicator's role in crisis is to be the central point of contact and source of knowledge inside and outside the company.

Now, my first question is always, "Has anyone been hurt?" Assessing the damage, especially impact on people, is fundamental. From there, I seek to understand the crisis at its source:

- What caused it?

- What can be done to fix it?

- How long will that take?

- How much more damage will occur in the meantime?

- What can my company do to help?

A strong communications leader will interrogate the problem and probe for what the public needs to know. Having a crisp understanding of the situation with a transparent timetable for updating the public is essential.

Open a command center. Proximity helps when dealing with a fast-moving disaster. During these pressure-cooker events, time is your enemy. So, there's real benefit in having all the experts in one room so that questions can be answered, and conflicts resolved, immediately. If the crisis is in a specific place (perhaps the result of a weather event), establish a team on the ground in the region. In the command center— or situation room, as it's sometimes called—be clear about roles and responsibilities. Yes, you will want to include a range of functions from digital to legal, from commercial to finance. But it's critical to know who is accountable for what and where decision rights rest.

Pull together in one place the technology, supplies, and support you will need over the hours and days to come. This may include everything from sophisticated social listening tools to plenty of water. Staying informed is essential, but hydration matters, too. Most importantly, the command center sends a signal that there is a place where the lights never go out, where the dangers of the crisis are addressed 24/7.

Create a stakeholder map. Each crisis has its own set of critical players, and no two crises are the same. On April 6, 1996, an Air Force CT-43 plane carrying my then-boss Secretary of Commerce Ron Brown along with thirty-four others, including Commerce Department colleagues and business leaders, crashed into a mountainside in Dubrovnik, Croatia. The tragedy was shocking and heartbreaking. The grim task for those leading the recovery effort included notification of family members about the loss of their loved ones. There is no more delicate task.

Typically, the stakeholder plan will include outreach to relevant regulatory authorities, perhaps other government officials. Most likely you'll have senior management, employees, and the board of directors on this list. Cast a wide net when compiling the names of those to inform. It's better to err on the side of being more inclusive with info rather than less.

Focus on the victims. Never let your focus waver from those who are impacted by the crisis. Remember that your needs will have to wait. During the BP oil spill, Hayward missed the mark. Initially he downplayed the spill, stating on May 17, 2010, that the environmental impact of the Gulf spill would be "very, very modest," and calling the spill "relatively tiny" in comparison with the vast ocean. In short order, Hayward had to reverse those remarks on CNN, declaring his company's actions an "environmental catastrophe." As I said earlier, he added to the communications damage done by later getting caught on video saying that "I would like to get my life back," while attending a yacht race off the Isle of Wight. Hayward later had to issue another apology for his insensitive comment, saying he was "deeply sorry" for his remark. Too little, too late. In June of that same year, Hayward lost his job.

Consider whether an apology is appropriate, and if the answer is yes, do it right. Be specific, addressing those impacted by name and reciting in no uncertain terms the offense. A weak apology is worse than none at all. Don't make it about you. Do not caveat the acknowledgment with "if I offended anyone . . ." Don't speak in vague, third-party terms. Owning one's action is essential.

A particularly bad apology was made by New York governor Andrew Cuomo in his resignation speech on August 10, 2021.[9] After being accused of harassment by at least eleven credible women, and months of stonewalling the charges, the governor finally decided to step down. When he did, he denied any wrongdoing and again tried to diminish the women's allegations that he inappropriately touched them or made sexually suggestive remarks by characterizing them as a political attack against him or just one big misunderstanding. Despite claiming to take "full responsibility," his apology was riddled with self-justifying excuses. Cuomo said, "In my mind, I have never crossed the line with anyone, but I didn't realize the extent to which the line has been redrawn." Those words did not cut it. This anemic apology demeaned the victims and failed to meet the standard of true remorse.

Visuals matter. The BP disaster was a story told in images. First, CNN ran a video feed continuously that showed oil dumping into the ocean. It was a persistent reminder of the spill's gravity. Like many watching in horror as the slick spread, I couldn't avert my eyes.

That gruesome visual was juxtaposed with Hayward yachting off the Isle of Wight just two days after facing a hostile congressional panel in an appearance that was widely panned as insensitive. President Barack Obama's chief of staff, Rahm Emanuel, chided Hayward's attendance at the yacht race as "part of a long line of PR gaffes and mistakes" on ABC television, saying, "I think that we can all conclude that Tony Hayward is not going to have a second career in PR consulting."

Imagine how the story may have been better with the image of executives hunkered around a conference table, sleeves rolled up. Or seeing the BP team out helping with the cleanup on the marred beaches in the coastal communities.

Finally, and I write more about this later, convey an appropriate level of propriety while dealing with crises. I keep a clean, pressed, somber dress ready to go in my offices both at work and at my home in case I'm called into action. I prefer not to find myself in front of TV cameras in the casual clothes that have become the style in corporate culture, and I certainly don't want to be scrambling for something decent to wear. Like it or not, these details matter.

Establish a rhythm. Determine the right cadence to update interested parties, especially the media. If possible, set a schedule whereby bulletins are issued twice daily, in the morning and at close of business. Remember this might be a marathon rather than a sprint, and managing your own energy will be important. See that your team rotates shifts to share the burden. No one can pull consecutive all-nighters and do good work. Needing sleep is not a weakness, it's a fact. I like to live by what I call "the oxygen mask rule." There's a good reason flight attendants say in the preflight announcements that should oxygen be required, you must put your own mask on before assisting small children. You aren't much good to anyone else if you don't take care of yourself.

Afterward, audit your crisis response. Before moving forward, take the time to debrief as a team. What did we do well? What can we do better next time? Most communications consulting firms offer crisis simulation exercises to practice and build your skills. As Mike O'Neill of American Express said to me, "The three most important things you can do to prepare for a crisis are train, train and train." It's worth the investment of time when things are calm to exercise your crisis muscles. When disaster strikes, you'll be glad you did.

These ideas represent first principles, your North Star when you're managing a crisis, not because they are revolutionary, but because they are effective.

CHAPTER SIX

Can You Hear Me Now?

Perfect Your Pitch

ON A SUNNY JUNE MORNING IN 2015, OUR DAUGHTER LILY asked whether we were going to the rally to hear Hillary Clinton launch her presidential bid on New York City's Roosevelt Island. I saw a light in her eyes. It meant something to her that we supported a woman who was seeking the nation's highest office, one who we genuinely admired.

"Of course, we're going! Let's get moving," I said. We grabbed our hats and sunscreen, pinned our campaign buttons to our shirts, and hopped on the nearest subway to join the crowd on Roosevelt Island.

There were many gals like me—women of a certain age—who were at the rally to support the candidate, to watch her make history. Our skulls were knotted from bumping up against all those glass ceilings.

We were Hillary's old faithfuls, pant-suited battle-axes with overprocessed hair and spreading waistlines—all those red-eye flights and client dinners had taken their toll. Our faces were timeworn. We were not Botox babes. We wore our wrinkles as badges of honor. We were Hillary people. My people. We may not be glamorous, but we're passionate, wizened professionals. Seeing us gathered, waiting for Hillary to take the podium with hopes held close made me tear up. There was something fierce and alive in our eyes, in our bellies. That day—with Hillary's announcement—we were taking a hill in the long battle.

When Hillary finally emerged from behind the curtain that bright day, the crowd surged. My daughter and I were carried with it. As Hillary walked down the elevated stage, we cheered her, calling her name. She waved back to the assembled, but it felt as though her gaze and greeting were directed at us, so personal were my feelings. We took photos and snapped selfies to remember the day we felt sure would be one for the record books.

As exciting as that rally was, almost as soon as her campaign started, Hillary's ship began to list. There were strategic fumbles and missed opportunities, in a voyage that seemed ill-fated from the start. She was overly cautious and seen as too centrist. She miscalculated the political math by not choosing a progressive like Elizabeth Warren as a running mate. Why? What was the problem? How could this woman with every possible achievement (scholar, lawyer, advocate, First Lady, senator, and secretary of state) be failing so badly? Why couldn't she connect with a constituency who was clearly fired up about the 2016 election?

My answer: Hillary lacked pitch.

This smart, savvy woman sounded small. She alienated and divided where she should have united and inspired. Despite Hillary's nonstop speaking engagements and media interviews, I believe no one was really hearing her, listening instead to what seemed like a stilted, detached discourse. She was not connecting; she wasn't breaking through.

The campaign hit rock bottom in September 2016 when, speaking at a fundraiser in New York City, Hillary said half of Donald Trump's supporters belong in a "basket of deplorables," characterized by "racist, sexist, homophobic, xenophobic, Islamophobic" views. Later in those remarks, Hillary tried to clean it up by adding that those people "feel that the government has let them down" and are "desperate for change. Those are people we have to understand and empathize with as well." But it was too late. The damage had been done. The "deplorables" comment echoed throughout the campaign and became a symbol of Hillary's supposed elitism—and an effective badge of honor for her detractors. While it may have been a clever and vivid comment, it was entirely lacking in pitch. It's not the sort of thing you say on the campaign trail. Failure to strike the right tone, one that connected with voters, dogged Hillary to the bitter end of her campaign.

On November 9, Hillary conceded before her supporters in a purple silk blouse meant to signal that, upon her election, she would bridge the divide between red and blue states. To me, in that difficult moment, the purple looked like a bad bruise. She was hurting and acknowledged as much. Early in her comments, she said, "I know how disappointed you feel, because I feel it too. This is painful and it will be for a long time." That comment struck me as vulnerable, revealing her humanity and tenderness in a way that, unfortunately, Hillary rarely allowed herself to be in the campaign.

She then confirmed that "Donald Trump will be our president and we owe him an open mind and a chance to lead." Here again she rose in these remarks to a higher plane, one not seen in the rough and tumble of the months that led to this moment. It might have helped if she had. That's statesmanship. Finally, at the conclusion of her comments— and here I teared up remembering the morning of her announcement on Roosevelt Island with our hopes held high—Hillary said, "And to all the little girls who are watching this, never doubt that you are valuable and powerful, and deserving of every chance and opportunity in the world to pursue and achieve your own dreams." That's the inspirational pitch that we listen for in our leaders.

Rising to a Moment

In contrast to Hillary's painful journey on the campaign trail, American Express CEO Ken Chenault achieved perfect pitch in the days following the September 11 attacks on the World Trade Center, next door to the company's lower Manhattan headquarters. Ken, retired from American Express since 2018, recounted for me the key moments and crucial communications and leadership lessons from the tragedy.

"On the morning of September 11, I was in a hotel in Salt Lake City, Utah, on a conference call with some members of my leadership team. They were in an office with windows overlooking the World Trade Center. I had the TV on with the sound off. Shortly after the start of the call, I literally saw the plane go into the building on the television screen as I heard the screams through the phone line of my colleagues who were witnessing the events. I was stunned. I was alone," Ken said.

He then made a series of urgent calls to his wife, to the headquarters in lower Manhattan where employees were evacuating, and to the regional operating center that he was visiting in Utah. Soon after, Ken established a crisis team to ensure that employees were safe, to source an alternative office space as nearly half the headquarters' building had been sheared off, and to mobilize customer service. Later that day, Ken reconvened his leadership team and told them, "Reputations are made or lost during times of crises."

"I knew I had to show compassion for the loss of life and also be decisive," Ken continued, emotion in his voice as he recounted his thoughts from twenty years earlier as if it was yesterday.

Initially unable to fly out of Salt Lake City, Ken gathered the local team for an informal dinner. He recalled feeling preoccupied that evening thinking of all that lay ahead. He was able to depart at 5 a.m.

the next morning and went to the temporary location just across the Hudson River in Jersey City that his real estate team had hustled to procure. There Ken stood up on top of a desk to address, support, and console the approximately two hundred employees from the tristate region who had gathered there. The following day Ken met with the families of the eleven American Express colleagues who had perished in the attack. "It was very emotional and important that I spend time with them," he said.

Over the next few days, Ken sent out employee videos and sent letters to impacted staff. He instinctually knew he needed to do more. "We needed the human connection. People needed to see me."

"Ken asked the question, 'When, how and where can we get together?' remembered Mike O'Neill, senior vice president for communications. "We scrambled to find a venue so we could bring more than five thousand people together in person. Finding a place in New York City one week after 9/11 was kind of a joke, but we knocked on enough doors until we found Madison Square Garden. With that decision taken, the security people went to work to make it as safe as possible, and the communication team found a way to reach out to five thousand people to get them to show up."

"I remember the night before I was thinking through what I was going to say. The team offered to prepare remarks, but I thought that would be too stilted. I scribbled a few notes that I eventually didn't use. I was nervous in the car ride to Madison Square Garden, but by the time I arrived, I knew exactly what I wanted to say and the importance of speaking from my heart," Ken said.

The singer Sheryl Crow sang a few songs to set the mood after which Ken took the stage and sat in a simple director's chair. "I told the assembled that our company is more than bricks and mortar, that American Express is represented by its people. I talked about our company values and how important they were in this moment. I talked about each of the colleagues who had been killed. I said that I understood their fear," he recalled. He also remembers taking a comment from a colleague who said that one of those who had lost his life had been a close friend. Ken waded into the audience and gave that man a hug.

Mike remembers Ken's concluding comment that day: "Our company is sound, our hearts are even stronger, and our minds will get clearer. We will overcome," he said. Unforgettable words from a leader under pressure. Ken's remarks had the core tenets of pitch: they united and inspired.

"It was so personal. So direct. It was a healing moment," Mike said. At the conclusion of Ken's remarks, Mike, who is not a demonstrative guy, went up and embraced him. He told Ken that "for a whole generation of people, this will be a dividing line between those who were here during this tragedy and the recovery, and those that joined afterward. It was that kind of powerful moment. We all understood that this was the day our comeback started."

To put the moment in context, Ken had only been CEO since January of that year. It had been a rough time in the business, and it was clear that the next year would be even tougher. Airplanes were not flying, and the travel industry that's so crucial to American Express was struggling. The economy was flat on its back.

"We would lose a fair amount of money during the period," Mike continued. "Still, Ken rose to the occasion. It was his company from that moment forward. There were sixty thousand people employed by American Express at the time and if you asked each one what they did at the company, they would reply, 'I work for Ken Chenault.'"

I was not working for American Express at the time, having left the year prior, so I wasn't in the auditorium. But Ken's pitch was so spot on that the words reverberated far beyond those in attendance. American Express alums like me and so many others were buoyed by Ken's confidence. That's the power of pitch done right.

I asked Ken what the most important advice was that he could offer to any leader communicating during a moment of unprecedented fear and anxiety. He said: "In a crisis it's very important to understand and express your core priorities. Where there is loss of life and a threat to someone's well-being and their future well-being, you've got to give them comfort and some rationale and emotions that they should have confidence. You need to be sure people see that you are emotionally impacted and reveal your vulnerabilities as well as your strengths. The mistake of some leaders in a crisis is that they don't show their empathy. If people feel you don't have empathy, you are not going to connect."

The Basics of Pitch

So, what exactly is pitch? The dictionary definition says it's "the quality of a sound governed by the rate of vibrations producing it; the degree of highness or lowness of a tone." But that doesn't really cut it for me. Pitch, in a leadership and communications context, is something much richer and more nuanced. It's the tenor, word choices, and attitude we bring to any human encounter. It's a striking of the right chords that allows us to reach and relate to one another more profoundly.

In 1964, Supreme Court Justice Potter Stewart delivered an opinion in the *Jacobellis v. Ohio* case with the now famous line related to the identification of pornography. "I know it when I see it," wrote the justice. A version of that is true for pitch. I know it when I hear it. Or better yet, I know it when I feel it, the connection and warmth it evokes. Pitch may be the single most vital element of successful communications that breaks through.

So, what are the core components of pitch? How can you achieve the timbre and tone that will distinguish you? The following are eight basic elements of pitch.

1. It's as simple as a smile. This precious gem of wisdom was bestowed on me by Dr. Melanie Katzman, renowned business psychologist, adviser, and consultant to the world's leading companies. Katzman

holds a doctorate in clinical psychology and maintains a private practice. She's also an entrepreneur with a highly successful consulting company that works with organizations and people in transitions. In her book, *Connect First: 52 Simple Ways to Ignite Success, Meaning, and Joy at Work*, the first chapter is titled, "Smile: Activate Immediate Connection." She explains that "when you smile at people, strangers included, 80 to 90 percent will return the gesture with a grin, even if they don't want to. . . . Even a well-placed forced smile is a mood enhancer."

I know many young people, and women especially, who resist smiling. I did. I thought I needed a tough look to send a signal of strength. I did not. It only made me look grumpy. It turned people off. In the media training I mentioned earlier with communications adviser Anita Dunn, she too told me about the power of a smile. During the video playback of my media training session, she said, "Do you see how, when you're thinking, your face rests naturally in a frown? We need to do something about that." I could see it. I looked angry even when I wasn't. My facial expression made me seem agitated, nervous, and defensive, not exactly the look I was aiming for. Now I've learned to arrange my face in a pleasant smile. Not a grinning Cheshire cat, but an expression of comfort and happiness to be engaged.

"Smiling is free and efficient. It asserts your intention to form a mutual, shared, equal connection. In challenging situations your smile can instantaneously, and often unconsciously, relax those around you," Katzman writes.

2. A positive attitude is essential. When First Lady Michelle Obama said in 2016, "When they go low, we go high," she instantly created a mantra for those who seek to stand above the fray of acrimony. In a *Time* magazine interview on November 20, 2018, the First Lady explained the meaning behind her now famous words. "'Going High' doesn't mean you don't feel the hurt, or you're not entitled to an emotion," she explained. "It means that your response has to reflect the solution. It shouldn't come from a place of anger or vengefulness. Barack and I had to figure that out. Anger may feel good in the moment, but it's not going to move the ball forward."

Moving the ball forward, in big ways and small, requires us to be purveyors of hope and optimism. This is something I try to do in my home. "Good morning, love," I trill from my home office each morning when the bedroom door cracks open and I hear my wife's feet pad toward the kitchen. I hope my few words convey my positivity for the day.

"Morning to you," she replies gently, as is her nature. This exchange establishes the mood in our home. In only those few first words spoken each day, we've set the pitch for the day and the vibe between us.

"Hello! Hello!" Albert bellows when he comes into the Pfizer office. It's not directed at a single individual, but to everyone within earshot. As chief executive, his warm and friendly tone puts everyone at ease.

3. Never talk down to people. Nothing is a bigger turn off than when someone is patronizing. Even if it's unintentional, it is annoying. It's also damaging to communications efforts because it's such a turn-off that people can dismiss the relevant parts of what you're saying. A guy who's a big deal in the public relations field runs one of the largest agencies in the business, wins many client pitches, and is generally considered a force within communications. I've known him a long time, and our families are friendly. Still, I see him almost entirely in professional settings. Without fail, he greets me with "Hi Kiddo!" My skin crawls every time. I'm a sixty-year-old woman with a decades-long career, a large team I lead, and a CEO who counts on me. I'm pretty sure he means it as an expression of affection. But it undercuts and roils. The next time I see him, I'm going to tell him.

I'll also do my best to ensure I'm not guilty of similar mistakes. In the corporate world, there can be a lot of hierarchy. One morning, I was entering our headquarters in Manhattan, and I waved to the security guard and said, "Hi, Hector." He looked up and replied,

"Good morning, Mrs. Susman." I was in a hurry, but I stopped for the necessary negotiation. "Listen, Hector," I said. "Either we both use first names, as in you call me Sally, or you'll need to let me know your surname and we can take the formal route." Hector gave me a warm, shy smile and said, "Okay, Sally, welcome to work." Until the Covid lockdown, we greeted one another casually each morning and evening. Hector died during the pandemic, and I miss him.

Companies can also be unwittingly condescending. In late 2015, Airbnb created several advertisements that it posted on bus kiosks and other places across San Francisco to protest the hotel taxes it paid, claiming they were excessive and weren't being used toward anything "important." One ad read, "Dear Public Library System, We hope you use some of the $12 million in hotel taxes to keep the library open later. Love, Airbnb." These ads sounded snarky. After public backlash, Airbnb issued a public apology and removed the offending ads.[1]

4. Mind the gap. That expression is used in London to warn you not to fall into the crevices between the subway (the Tube) and the platform. It is one of many unique uses of the English language that I learned while living and working there in the mid-1990s. I quickly came to understand what playwright George Bernard Shaw meant when he said Britain and the United States are "two countries divided by a common language."

When I first moved to London, I was late to several appointments before I realized that my American understanding of the "first floor" being at ground level was different from the English tradition of that being the floor above the entry level. And it went downhill for me from there, with so many opportunities for misunderstanding. My colleague once told me my boss "came back from lunch pissed." I worried that he was angry, only to learn that for the Brits that meant he was drunk. These are just a few examples to make the point that it is necessary to pause and understand the context to ensure a meeting of the minds.

When businesses attempt to reach customers from other cultures, which is increasingly necessary to succeed in a global marketplace, it's crucial they understand cross-cultural differences. If we are not aware of the impact of communications errors on cross-cultural relations, the misunderstandings can cause serious damage to those efforts. Pringles, the crisp snack, and Tesco, the British supermarket chain, both failed when a special Ramadan holiday display featuring bacon-flavored chips was promoted in stores.[2] While the chips didn't actually contain pork, it was incredibly ignorant to create such a display, and both companies faced legitimate criticism. Be aware of, and sensitive to, communications gaps that can be rooted in regional, social, cultural, or generational differences.

5. Align communications with corporate culture. A leader and breakthrough communicator must make sure her vocabulary matches the corporate culture she operates in. If your company is striving to be innovative and agile, be sure your sentences are short and punchy. Avoid long rambling sentences or endless paragraphs. Be strategic and cautious around humor. I write more about this slippery slope in chapter 8. If your company is highly regulated and depends on exacting quality and safety standards, be careful not to use overly casual or cheeky language, which is not to say you should stick to business speak; you shouldn't. It does mean you should be mindful of the culture you're in, and its proprieties, when speaking.

An example of different cultural nuances is the various ways that companies refer to the people they employ. At Pfizer, we say "colleagues." The Ritz-Carlton calls its workers "ladies" or "gentlemen" to convey respect to those in service positions. Jet Blue uses the term "crewmember," typically reserved for folks who work in flight. But it has extended it to its entire workforce, from mechanic to executive, to create an egalitarian feeling. Disney employees are called "cast members," and Taco Bell calls its cashiers "champions." When Facebook named itself Meta, it changed the terminology for its employees from the well-known Facebookers to Metamates.

The first time I heard Leonard Lauder call me "darling," I was startled. But I came to understand and appreciate that such expressions of familiarity were aligned with the culture of that family business. Likewise, he insisted I call him Leonard, and at first it was a struggle for me not to refer to him as Mr. Lauder. In time, I managed it.

6. Locate your unique voice, tone, and cadence. I'm a follower of Adam Grant, an organizational psychologist at Wharton and bestselling author. On October 13, 2021, Grant posted the following on LinkedIn: "Don't confuse being a fast talker with being a deep thinker. Speaking quickly signals confidence, not complexity. Don't mistake volume for expertise. Speaking loudly reflects conviction more than credibility." These are wise words and relieving ones for me, as I am a slow talker who rarely raises her voice.

I've worked to tune my own authentic voice and pacing. I hope to be received as calm, welcoming, and measured (important in my profession, where crises are around every corner). I don't always achieve that goal, but it's my ambition.

I try to infuse my emails with a pleasant tone. I start them with a friendly salutation like a "Good afternoon" or a simple "Hi there," just to signal a humane hello before diving into my request or response. Those small touches warm and personalize the note. This is especially relevant for emails and texts, which can often be transactional with much lost in translation.

One way to locate your voice is to listen for those who speak most directly to you. For me, writer and film director Nora Ephron's voice is one I wish to emulate. Jewish, born in New York City, raised in Hollywood, the eldest of four sisters, Ephron's wit and brilliance ring through her work. She is best known for her romantic comedy film *When Harry Met Sally* and for the autobiographical novel *Heartburn* based on her marriage to and divorce from journalist Carl Bernstein. She was dedicated to her craft. Via the HBO documentary on Ephron titled *Everything Is Copy*, we learn that the title is the mantra she learned from her mother, also a writer. Nothing is off-limits, and that "no holds barred" way of expressing herself drew me in. As a reader, I believed Ephron let me into her hurting heart to find strength in her resilience.

Another voice I relate to is Elizabeth Gilbert's, author of *Eat Pray Love, The Signature of All Things*, and *Big Magic: Creative Living Beyond Fear*, which I recommend to anyone considering an artistic pursuit. Gilbert and I have never met, but her voice is so clear to me that I feel as though we are friends. In my fantasized conversations with her, I call her Liz. It's worth listening to the voices that speak to you. Know them, befriend them in your mind, and seek to emulate them.

Regarding accents, I've seen many an executive tortured by elocution training that I believe is largely unnecessary. Unless one's accent is so overwhelming as to render one incomprehensible, I wouldn't worry about it. I like the way Estée Lauder Companies' chief executive Fabrizio Freda's Italian accent lends an old-world charm to his speeches. Albert Bourla has a thick Greek accent that adds to his authenticity and reminds people that we are a truly global company. I've lived in New York for nearly thirty years, and in Washington and London before that, but every so often, especially when I'm tired, my Midwestern drawl will creep into my speech with its nasal twang and a tendency to elongate vowels, particularly the A. I don't mind. It's where I'm from and who I am.

7. Be conversational. A real meeting of the minds happens when dialogue is shared, with ideas flowing back and forth. Being conversational is like dancing seamlessly when neither party dominates the other and the partners move together. In communications, we achieve that flow when we work as hard to listen as to speak. It's a rhythm required for pitch between people.

I saw the antithesis of a true, mutual dialogue when I started my first job on Capitol Hill. During my breaks from the mailroom, I liked to sit in the Senate galleries and listen to the debate. One day a senator was droning on for hours. It made no sense to me. I asked the guard what was happening, and he explained to me what it meant to filibuster.

In the US Senate, a filibuster is an act of obstructionism whereby a person speaks at inordinate length to block a legislative measure with the goal of preventing its final passage into law. It's a delaying tactic and one of the oddest things I've ever seen. A person talks and talks, reading from the phone book or any kind of endless narrative. Minority members have used the filibuster when they had no other choice. Southern Democrats led by Senator Richard Russell held up the Civil Rights Act of 1964 for sixty working days. Thankfully, in the end, this ploy failed, but not before infuriating a lot of people and wasting a fair amount of time. Beware of someone droning on, hogging the microphone, or dominating discussion. They may not be formally filibustering, but they are obstructing the honest exchange of ideas. Blowhards never achieve pitch.

Also, being conversational is not disrespectful. This is a misconception I carried for a long time and a mistake I see many people make—believing that language needs to be formal to be respectful. These poor souls use big, complex words or convolute their sentences when speaking. They tend to overwrite in written communications. It's not necessary or helpful. If you can say it simply, do so.

8. End on a high note. As a former White House press secretary and current co-anchor of *America's Newsroom* on Fox News Channel, Dana Perino is someone I admire for her wit, wisdom, and upbeat attitude. In her memoir, *And the Good News Is . . . : Lessons and Advice from the Bright Side*, Perino underscores the virtue in looking for the silver linings. No matter how hard a briefing was to deliver to President Bush, and during her tenure there were some dark days for the Bush White House, she found something hopeful to say in the end. Perino explained to me that the "good news" might be her plans to mitigate the negative publicity, or a proactive approach to offer a rebuttal, or sometimes even just a healthy dose of some comforting context. Her goal in highlighting the hopeful elements was to always leave her principal believing in her and her abilities, and ultimately wanting more advice and counsel.

Now that Perino is no longer at the White House and has a celebrated show each morning, I asked her if she still thinks a lot about her tone.

She said, "I do. For myself, I'm cautious in my words. I also want to have fun and the confidence that I'm being responsible, and fact based. So, yes, to be effective in public facing communications you want to have grace and dignity because people are more likely to listen. You're more likely to be persuasive and get the kind of response that you want from your audience if you can find a ray of optimism." And that's the good news.

The irony about pitch is that, in some circumstances, it can have a negative connotation. Nobody wants to be pitched by a publicist just smiling-and-dialing with no real commitment to the product or service she is promoting. No one wants to feel pitched by an aggressive salesperson in a boutique telling you something looks good on you when it doesn't. I don't want to hear the fundraising pitch by a candidate with whom I have no connection. And my least favorite notion is the famous "elevator pitch," where aspiring individuals are encouraged to make their case in the time it takes to ride from the ground floor of a building to the penthouse. Sure, sometimes we find ourselves under pressure to get to the point or to make a sale, but that kind of extreme pressure is rare. I don't like the stress it puts on people, especially younger folks or those just starting out in the work world.

More often than not, you will want to refine your message in a way that allows your unique and engaging style—or pitch—to emerge. Be remembered as being the one who listened carefully and then asked astute questions, who took in the environment and made a thoughtful observation, who was self-aware enough to know when the conversation had run its natural course, or who had a finely tuned ear to know just the right moment to lift her voice and make her mark.

CHAPTER SEVEN

Hey! Who's Going to Get the Credit?

Disarm with Humility,
Empower with Truth

WHEN MY NIECE CAROLYN WAS ABOUT FIVE YEARS OLD, I took her out early one summer morning to teach her to fish. Just after dawn we climbed into the family Jeep, an old blue model with faux wood paneling on the sides. We drove to a freshwater pond near Nantucket's cranberry bogs. I had packed two poles, some minnows for bait, and red-and-white plastic bobbers to go on our lines so we could see when the fish were biting. We found a good spot on the water, a weathered but sturdy wooden dock, and hooked our bait. "Spit on the minnow for good luck," I said, just as my grandfather had instructed me to do when I was her age. We lowered our lines into the cold water and waited. And then waited some more.

"Jiggle your pole," I said. For more than three hours I offered Carolyn every technique I knew to lure a fish. We had no luck. Not even a nibble. I imagined we were going to have to pack it in and go home without anything to show for our efforts. Then, as we were about to call it quits, Carolyn's bobber plunged underwater, and her line went taut. "Reel him in slowly," I whispered, and she did exactly that. With a steady hand, Carolyn landed a small fish. I snapped a photo of her, holding her prized catch in two hands and with an enormous grin on her face. We decided to let the little fellow live. Carolyn carefully unhooked him and slipped him back into the pond.

"You caught your first fish!" I said to my niece as we headed home.

"No, Aunt Sally, *we* caught the fish," Carolyn said.

I've never forgotten that tender moment of humility expressed by a young girl. How easily that modest and authentically inclusive comment rolled off her tongue. How humility is a sign of strength and confidence rather than weakness. How rare it is to find a genuinely humble soul like that these days.

Many large multinational companies are perceived as lacking humility. This is not a surprising conclusion to reach. Read their press releases or annual reports and you'll see that it's far more likely that big corporations are boastful and self-satisfied, as if arrogance is in their DNA. Bragging about performance does not add to market value, so it's not a good business decision. It can diminish it. A 2021 study published in the *Journal of Corporate Finance* found that boasting about performance is not associated with value creation. In fact, the study found that firms that did not boast about earnings enjoyed stronger financial performance over their less humble peers.[1]

For these reasons and others, the counterintuitive first step Pfizer took at the beginning of the pandemic was noteworthy. On March 13, 2020, just days after the World Health Organization declared the global pandemic, Pfizer issued a "Five-Point Collaboration Plan" calling on the biopharmaceutical industry to join us in committing to unprecedented cooperation to combat Covid-19. The public call to action was brainstormed by Albert Bourla, the scientific and legal teams, and my communications group. Ed Harnaga, a talented senior member of my team with a strong grounding in science, held the pen as we tossed ideas around. Ultimately our collaboration plan included five promises ranging from sharing our tools and insights to offering our manufacturing capabilities to others, including competitors, all focused on "helping scientists more rapidly bring forward therapies and vaccines to protect humankind from this escalating pandemic and prepare the industry to better respond to future global health crises." It was a groundbreaking declaration that set the tone for all our public statements going forward. Humility was our watchword. A sense of community and collaboration guided us. "The only enemy is the virus," was our mantra. It was an "all for one and one for all" moment, too rarely expressed or seen in corporate America.

Fast forward to the fall of 2021. Two companies, Pfizer and Moderna, had developed and produced novel mRNA vaccines and began to supply the world. For reasons I will never understand, Moderna started sending arrows our way. We heard from key opinion leaders and journalists that, essentially, Moderna's top executives were trashing us. Their digs and insults hit a low point when on October 29, 2021, Bloomberg ran a story following an editorial meeting with Moderna's top brass.[2] The headline: "Pfizer Won the First Round, But Moderna Sees Final Victory Ahead." Moderna charged that Pfizer was only "dabbling" in the new and exciting mRNA technology. It attempted to ridicule us for our size. Moderna president Stephen Hoge is quoted as saying, "For the extra, whatever it is, 78,000 people, how come they are only a month ahead." The article is a litany of whines and competitive complaints from Moderna.

Did we throw a counterpunch? Did we brag about the ways we felt we had achieved more than Moderna? No. Our spokeswoman, Amy Rose, said, "We have all worked tirelessly and collaboratively to combat the Covid-19 global health crisis, as we have known from the very beginning that it would take the efforts of more than one company to fight this deadly virus. At Pfizer, we're proud of all that we've done but we're equally proud of what our peers have accomplished too." We honored the contributions of others. We employed the wisdom that my little niece knew when it came to claiming credit for catching a fish. We refused to take the bait (pun intended). The world recognized our humility and saw it as a demonstration of our steadiness and grit during the Covid crisis. We continued to lead the industry in positive impressions. Our stature among elected officials and the general public was riding high.[3]

At the risk of sounding immodest in this chapter on humility, there were so many times during our pandemic response that Pfizer took the high road. The vista is beautiful from up there. The clouds of division are clear, and the path forward is in sight. The clarity that comes once you've stopped pursuing the false god of credit-claiming is an enormous leadership and communications asset. A modest demeanor opens others to hear you and to align with your mission. Humility is most disarming when it's exercised by the very powerful. Great leaders that I admire are some of the humblest people. The unexpected nature of their modesty is hugely attractive, and it has currency.

The mogul. I had the chance to meet Warren Buffett when he was a speaker at a conference for women in business. Along one of the long corridors of the hotel hosting the conference, I spotted him, the chairman and CEO of Berkshire Hathaway, a man considered one of the most successful investors in the world with a net worth of over $100 billion.

He was walking alone, without an entourage of aids or a security detail. I went up to shake his hand and say hello, as did many other women attending the program. He stopped to talk to each of us, asking us questions about our work, ambitions, or families. He was genuine, humble, and so understated that if you didn't know he was a business magnate, you might have thought he was someone's uncle who had wandered in off the street. But do not be fooled by Buffett's modesty or frugality. He's a force who knows the power of giving it all away. The man known in investing circles as the "Oracle" or the "Sage" has long pledged to give away 99 percent of his wealth.[4]

I'm convinced that much of Buffett's influence emanates from self-effacing humility. People listen to him because he doesn't make big promises or unrealistic claims. Buffett's investing advice is clear and sound, delivered in an understated and pragmatic fashion. So, it's hard to believe that at one time, he had a paralyzing fear of public speaking. To overcome it, at just age nineteen, he enrolled in a Dale Carnegie speech preparation and execution course.[5] As a result, he is a virtuoso storyteller, able to make financial concepts understandable and actionable that others in the field go out of their way to make sound mysterious and complex.[6]

The former president. When President Carter failed to be reelected in 1980, it looked as if history would relegate him to the bottom of the presidential heap and declare him the least effective president in modern history. He was criticized for failing to deal with the energy crisis, blamed for runaway price inflation, and trashed for failing to free American hostages in Iran. I assumed that after being dumped by American voters, Carter would go back to his hometown, Plains, Georgia, and that would be the last we'd hear from him. Boy, was I wrong.

Embracing a spirit of humility, Carter rose in his post-presidency like a phoenix. He found his voice and connected with people in ways he had not previously achieved. It began when, following his election defeat, Carter told the White House press corps that he wanted to follow in the footsteps of President Harry Truman and not capitalize on his time in the White House to enrich himself. Rather he and his wife, Rosalynn, dedicated themselves to quieter, personal, and phil-anthropic pursuits including swinging a hammer and banging nails to build houses as longtime volunteers, advocates, and fundraisers for Habitat for Humanity, and founding The Carter Center to advance human rights and alleviate human suffering in more than eighty countries. And, in his spare time, he wrote thirty-two books!

I've read many of these books and find Carter's values of humility and principles of generosity both deeply moving and instructive. Carter's legacy is now being reappraised, and deservedly so. His unwavering commitment to human rights, his attention to policy and legislative details, and his devotion to his wife (the couple celebrated their seventy-fifth wedding anniversary in 2021) are among the positive attributes we hear about the former president today. *Washington Monthly* magazine wrote a piece in its November 2021 issue titled "The Surprising Greatness of Jimmy Carter." It's never too late for the humble to be seen, heard, and appreciated.

The anthropologist. Dame of the British Empire, and recipient of countless honorary degrees and global recognition awards, including 2021 winner of the Templeton Prize in recognition of her life's work on animal intelligence and humanity, primatologist and anthropologist Jane Goodall built her reputation on the study of chimpanzees in Tanzania in the 1960s. But her legacy will last not only because of her expertise but because of her humble service to both animals and humankind. After a record-breaking fifty years of continuous study of chimpanzee behavior in their natural habitat, she continues to focus much of her time on the eponymous Jane Goodall Institute, specifically on the Roots and Shoots program, an environmental and humanitarian education program for young people, which encourages them to take action on conservation issues in their own communities. There is no need for her to run such a program, but she does it anyway, with very little fanfare for herself. Indeed, when she walks into a university or other gathering place to give a speech, she is rarely recognized until she is introduced at the podium.

The humble man's antithesis is the braggart. We all know someone who is a boaster and a blowhard—the colleague who takes all the credit or the politician who overstates his accomplishments. What the braggart may not realize is that his exaggerations and inflation of the truth severely undermine his credibility.

Let's review the case of NBC news anchor Brian Williams. Early in his career, Williams was admired for his work ethic, reporting skills, and straightforward, down-home style. He made his way from his first broadcasting gig at KOAM-TV in Pittsburg, Kansas, to become the *NBC Nightly News* anchor in 2004, arguably the most powerful position in TV news. His humble, boyish charm was part of his appeal. He was credibility personified.

All that trustworthiness was squandered when, in 2015, Williams was forced to apologize on air for a fabricated story he told for years about a close call on a helicopter on a US mission in Iraq. His version of events had shifted over the years. Originally, Williams reported the incident truthfully: a helicopter traveling thirty minutes ahead of Williams's was hit by a rocket-propelled grenade. Williams didn't see the chopper get hit, but over time the account morphed to the point where he said he was aboard the attacked aircraft as it took ground fire. When this discrepancy was revealed, other accounts from Williams's reportage, especially those that included himself, came under scrutiny. "There are questions swirling about his accounts from the aftermath of Hurricane Katrina, centered around his claims to have witnessed a suicide inside the Superdome and a dead body floating by his hotel in New Orleans. . . . [T]he *Washington Post* reported that Williams has given different accounts from his reporting on the 2006 Israel-Hezbollah war," reported Money.CNN.com.[7]

Following these revelations of overblown claims, Williams was suspended. After a period of sitting on the sidelines, he came back on air on MSNBC's *The 11th Hour with Brian Williams* show. It was a comeback, but Williams never had the same level of authority or implied integrity that he previously enjoyed. Williams's need to bolster his claims, exaggerate his experiences, and place himself at the center of the story devastated his credibility and undermined his moral authority. Near the end of 2021, Williams retired. I'm willing to bet that now, in hindsight, he deeply regrets the times he wandered off the path of truthfulness in the pursuit of self-aggrandizement.

I get it. I am not a stranger to the urge to stretch the truth. As a young girl, I told lies. Some were skinny little ones, while others were big fat whoppers. To strangers, I introduced myself under my favorite pseudonym, Jennifer. To neighbors, I audaciously claimed that I had a cool older brother who lived in a treehouse in our backyard.

I compounded one lie right on top of another, creating a deceitful domino effect. Once, in a dramatic display in front of my sixth-grade classroom, I miraculously "found" my missing and overdue assignment behind the teacher's filing cabinet—having slipped it there moments earlier. "Look, Mrs. Kercher, you must have dropped my assignment behind the drawers," I said. The truth was I'd simply failed to turn my work in on time. I had a self-sabotaging streak in those days.

Having been born a long time before yesterday, Mrs. Kercher did not fall for my act and marched me off to the principal's office, where I broke down in tears. I explained to the principal that I'd perpetrated the fraud because I was devastated from having been recently diagnosed with a terminal illness. He stared at me—the picture of perfect health—and phoned my parents. My dad came to the school, picked me up, and we drove home in stony silence. He and my mother were furious.

Clearly, I was not a very skilled liar, and my mother almost always caught me. She'd come down hard, voicing her anger, jabbing her forefinger at me for emphasis, and glaring in disappointment. "There are no liars in this family," Mom said. In her book, perjury was a criminal offense.

I'm not completely sure why I did it. Sometimes I'd create a sad story, such as the serious illness of a nonexistent friend, to engender sympathy.

Other times I added drama to paint a romantic image of myself, conjuring an imaginary boyfriend who would be with me if he were not being held hostage by terrorists in a foreign county.

Mainly I fabricated and falsified because I thought I needed something more. I lied to defend myself against pedestrian sameness. Fearful that me, myself, and I would not suffice, I embellished my suburban life to scrub away its perceived mundanity. I suspect that's why others do it too. Perhaps an insecurity lies at the heart of every boastful, overblown claim. This was true for me as a child and was likely the case for Brian Williams, even as he sat in one of the most powerful chairs, that of NBC news anchor. I learned over time, and through embarrassing revelations of my hyperbole, that inflating the truth is a surefire trust buster. Ironically, the untruths told to make oneself seem bigger render us smaller. The attempt to build oneself up tears you down. It's a losing game.

One of the unfortunate aspects of social media is that it enables bragging and can create an idealized vision of a life that seems perfect but is not real.[8] Individuals and corporations are guilty of using social platforms to depict utopias that are unattainable. Humblebragging, a form of self-promotion that tries, unsuccessfully, to hide a brag within self-deprecation is rampant. Are we fooled by someone who posts, "Can't believe someone as clumsy as I am managed to run the marathon" or "Huge promotion at work! Just reached six figures. #blessed"? Let's resist the temptation to stretch the truth in our communications and avoid bragging through phony complaints about ourselves.

By contrast, sincerity, an outer-directed spirit, and an ego kept in check make for a more admirable, persuasive leader and communicator. Having a truly humble, transparent, and truthful approach is crucial. I had to draw on these traits to achieve the most important duty I had during the vaccine rollout, that of encouraging the public to have faith in the new vaccine and to receive it with confidence. It wasn't easy.

Commit to Hearing the Other Point of View

In the summer of 2020, I met up with a friend at the beach on Long Island, outdoor socializing being the only way to get together at that time. We stood at the windy water's edge and talked. This is a smart and thoughtful person, someone whom I respect and admire. When she told me emphatically, perhaps forgetting what I did or whom I worked for, that there "was no way I'll take that vaccine for a couple of years because we won't know enough about it," my initial reaction was a desire to push her into the icy waves. Instead, I paused and decided to listen. That conversation made me realize that it wasn't just the faceless "public" who would be skeptical about the vaccine, but people I knew, loved, and respected might have legitimate worries and understandable hesitation. I had to check my assumptions about how people perceived the vaccine at a time when they were already stressed about the potential of getting the virus, losing their jobs, and wondering what the future held. I needed to take these concerns seriously—all of them, from everyone—and respect their worries and anxiety, and make a genuine effort to walk in their shoes.

In the spirit of empathy and respect, I rejected the name-calling and refused to label skeptics "anti-vaxxers," because it is alienating and aggressive and puts people on the defense. That's not where you want them to be to have a rational discussion about medicine and health. It also wasn't an accurate name, because many of the people who were questioning the Covid vaccine had children who were fully vaccinated against serious childhood diseases, trusted doctors, and understood the lifesaving value of pharmaceuticals.

As a breakthrough communicator, I chose instead to listen to the concerns, ask questions, and see things from their perspective—all essential to dramatically boosting vaccine confidence rates. It was how we, as a global society, began to change the trajectory of the caseload and start to reopen the world. All good communications are exercises in sharing knowledge in a way that makes the receivers feel comfortable and respected. Empathy is not a magical quality that only a few possess. Most human beings can relate; we may have to remember to use it and we should anytime we are trying to lead change. Empathy enables communication with the unwilling, the skeptical, and the distracted.

With a few notable exceptions that I'll touch on later, my feeling was that those who were reluctant to vaccinate wouldn't be moved or persuaded by national political figures, rock stars, or celebrities. Rather, the power to persuade was with those closer by—the teacher, the preacher, the barber, the neighbor. Experience bore that out. I listened as my wife chatted with the vaccine-hesitant lady behind the checkout counter at our local liquor store until she felt comfortable taking the shot. And I was able to convince that friend of mine whom I met at the shoreline to get vaccinated by simply answering her questions, one by one, over several months. We succeed in these encounters not by counting them as wins and losses but by meeting one another as fellow humans.

In that spirit, in January of 2021 and in collaboration with American Nurses Association, National Black Nurses Association, American Pharmacists Association, American College of Emergency Physicians, American College of Preventive Medicine, and our partner BioNTech, Pfizer developed a public service campaign to encourage the public to think about their reasons for vaccination. Our goal was not to fight with facts but move hearts with emotion and empathy. We were not going to bully or intimidate, but instead we wanted to understand and embrace the questions and doubts people had.

Each public service announcement (PSA) was a fifteen- to thirty-second vignette that used actual home movies of tender moments. There's the woman announcing she is pregnant by saying, "There's a bun in the oven," passing her sonogram photo to a family hanging out on a sofa, and her mother explodes with joy. There's another where two twenty-something friends embrace in a long-overdue hug with the tagline "You can't do this on a screen." In another, we see a seventy-four-year-old grandfather cuddling with his one-year-old granddaughter for their first playdate. In the fourth in the series, a young father going to work says goodbye to his young son through the forced separation of a glass door. The PSA asks the question, "Why will you get vaccinated?" We recognized that everyone has their own reason. There was no one universal answer to that provocation, just a collection of raw emotion.

These deeply personal PSAs drove more than 178,000 unique visitors to our SciencePossible website created for the campaign. For comparison, this is greater than the response to some of the websites for Pfizer's branded medicines, which were advertising during the same period with greater resources and longer campaigns. These messages received more than $2.4 million in donated outdoor advertising space (i.e., billboards) secured by our creative agency, in Atlanta, Baltimore, Boston, Cleveland, Dallas, Denver, Detroit, Houston, and Los Angeles.

The National Basketball Association donated TV time throughout its 2021 season for the PSAs, which played during games on NBA TV, ESPN, and TNT. By the end of June, local TV stations aired the PSAs over 6,000 times generating an estimated 110 million impressions. On Facebook, Twitter, Instagram, and LinkedIn, the ads performed very well against the benchmarks, from a diverse audience across the country.

Hone Humility

How do we drop the cloak of arrogance and get in the right frame of mind to engage with humility? What are the best tactics that prepare us to be humble leaders? How do we lay down arms and forgo our competitive instincts to reach a collective consensus?

You may have noticed that much of the advice I'm offering here is lessons I've gleaned from my parents, my wife, and my friends. That renders them no less valid than if they came from the best communications or leadership programs at an Ivy League institution. Much of the communications craft is learned through life lessons. Humility may be taught in the classrooms of daily living. Here are a few suggestions.

Share the limelight. Before the pandemic, Pfizer didn't do much corporate advertising. Most of our marketing had been conducted on behalf of our brand-name medicines. When Covid emerged, the smart brand marketers at Pfizer realized that it could appear tone-deaf to promote our brands at a time when many doctor's offices were closed and hospital emergency rooms were overrun. As a result, there was TV advertising space that had been purchased that could have gone unused. A perfectly good ad buy is a terrible thing to waste, so my team swung into action. We hopped on a call with Grey Group, an advertising agency, and quickly shuffled draft language back and forth. The words needed to be urgent and original. This campaign wasn't about promoting brands or even trumpeting the virtues of Pfizer. Rather, we needed a sixty-second TV spot that celebrated science and gave hope. We named it "Science Will Win." It was written in the spirit of one of the rules I had learned long ago from my mom: "Don't toot your own horn."

In the TV ad, the narrator says,

> At a time when things are most uncertain, we turn to the most certain thing there is: science. Science can overcome diseases, create cures, and yes, beat pandemics. It has before, it will again because when it's faced with a new opponent, it doesn't back down, it revs up, asking questions until it finds what it's looking for. That's the power of science. So, we're taking our science and unleashing it, our research, experts, and resources, all in an effort to advance potential therapies and vaccines. Other companies and academic institutions are doing the same. The entire

> global scientific community is working together to beat this thing, and we're using science to help make it happen because when science wins, we all win.

The hero in this commercial wasn't my company, but scientists everywhere. The response was awesome. More than 1 billion people saw this advertisement—750 million from our television and digital ad buy and another 250 million from those who shared the segment on their social media channels.

This simple phrase—Science Will Win—became our mantra, and we said it at the end of many meetings during our race for the vaccine, like a cheer. It was even a fashion statement. We used it to adorn face masks and T-shirts.

Most importantly, the Science Will Win position surprised people. We spent precious resources acknowledging someone other than ourselves. We shared the limelight, and it reflected well on us.

Own your mistakes. When the National Basketball Association was trying to get all players vaccinated before the start of the 2021–2022 season, several, including Kyrie Irving of the Brooklyn Nets, said they would not and were "doing their own research." Because of his unvaccinated status, Irving was unable to play for the Nets in their first preseason game. While doing his own research could include talking to his doctor, Irving had been pushing vaccine conspiracies about topics including microchips in the vaccine. In his audio commentary during the Rockets game, the former coach and current NBA commentator Jeff Van Gundy questioned whether this "research" was legitimate.

Van Gundy tweeted, "You know the one that drives me crazy? 'I'm doing my own research.' I would like someone to answer the question: What does that look like?"

Late in the evening on October 9, 2021, my team recommended that we retweet Van Gundy's quote via @thecrossover, *Sports Illustrated*'s streaming podcast. The blowback was swift; we had 162 highly negative comments on the post in the first twelve hours, the majority of which referenced misinformation directly related to antibodies and fetal stem cells. Moving quickly to address our mistake, we deleted the retweet on October 9 due to the negative sentiment rather than our original intention of calling attention to someone (Kyrie Irving) who was the victim of misinformation.

Not everything lands well, especially on social media. When we see a pattern of negative sentiments in response to social media posts, it may be the right decision to remove the post. It's not easy to experiment in public in real time, and not a good idea, but sometimes we make mistakes when we are reacting to acute events that are happening in the moment. Doing so makes me uncomfortable, but we often have to endure trial and error in the public square to find the right recipe for social media and succeed at it. I've done my best to adopt a live-and-learn mentality, and I make sure to pivot appropriately and rationally when missteps happen.

"The only bad mistake is one you stick by," my father told me on many occasions. I keep these words in mind because I make mistakes. Don't we all. If we are not regularly failing, perhaps we aren't trying hard enough.

Find truth-tellers. Find friends who are willing to give you some tough love. Once you meet them, work hard to keep them close. My core posse consists of two friends I made in Washington, DC, in my midtwenties, Hilary Rosen and Lisa Sherman. We've been through highs (weddings, adoptions, promotions) and lows (breakups, ailing parents, work debacles, and more).

Hilary is the former vice chair of the public affairs firm SKDKnickerbocker, and Lisa is the CEO of the Advertising Council, so not only are they beloved by me, but they are widely recognized for their wisdom and experience. Both are celebrated in their fields. What I most appreciate is their willingness to be honest with me, sometimes brutally so. We have a bond of loyalty. If I type 9-1-1 into a text, my posse comes running. It comforts me to know if I send up a flare, they will be there. Always.

And I do the same for them. Why does having truth-tellers help? In the spring of 2012, Hilary, the communications expert, made a rare misstep on national TV. The presidential campaign was in full swing, and both sides were angling to win the women's vote. President Barack Obama held a lead. Challenger Mitt Romney often invoked his wife, Ann, as his link to issues women faced in the economy. Hilary, a top-ranked surrogate speaker for team Obama, ignited a firestorm when she countered on CNN that Ann Romney "never worked a day in her life." Hilary was immediately and widely rebuked for taking a swing at a candidate's family member and stoking the division between moms who work inside and outside the home. It hurt to see my friend criticized in public. I knew she was smarting, and I reached out to offer solace and support. But she needed more than solace. As she and I have discussed more recently, some of us are highly capable of dispensing excellent advice, but not as talented when it comes to our own mistakes. Despite the old adage, it is hard for a doctor to heal herself.

At first, Hilary tried to publicly explain her comment. She wrote an opinion piece for *Huffington Post*. The doubling down didn't help. Even though this started as a defense of President Obama, he and the First Lady distanced themselves from Hilary's comment. "I don't have a lot of patience for commentary about the spouses of political candidates," said the president. "Every mother works hard; every woman deserves to be respected—MO," chimed in Michelle Obama through a tweet.

So what do you do when you see someone standing in a wreck? I pushed and told her she needed to apologize. She was reluctant at first and, I believe, felt taken advantage of by the Republicans and unsupported by the Democrats. After a couple of frank conversations, she relented, and within twenty-four hours of making the offending comment, Hilary apologized to Ann Romney for "her poorly chosen words," and said we should put "the faux war against stay-at-home moms to rest once and for all." Former First Lady Barbara Bush came to the rescue, commended Hilary's apology, and said people should "forget it." This whole issue made a lot of news at the time and then went away. But it is relevant here to show that it is actually possible to reverse a bad public decision and move on if you have the right humility and the right advice. When a communications crisis hits, it's hard to find new advisers in the moment, so make sure you have your truth-tellers on hand.

In a painful truth-telling moment, Lisa confronted me over a draft speech I'd written and asked her to review for an occasion where we would both be speaking. She called me at home on a Sunday afternoon. From her first hello, I could feel tension on the line. Apparently, my draft was full of views she and I had shared, and it cut too close to her remarks. She told me so in no uncertain terms. I was embarrassed and annoyed that Lisa felt I'd taken her ideas, and that our comments from the same stage would be repetitive if I didn't change my script. I had no choice but to start again. I wrote a more original and authentic speech. In hindsight, Lisa had been right, and my comments had been too close to hers. I'm thankful she had the courage and candor to point it out.

Neither moment was comfortable, but both were catalytic, and we helped one another be stronger. Over the years, our courage to confront each other has made us not only better people, but more powerful advocates for the causes we care about.

So, yes, loyal, truth-telling friends can make you a better communicator. What should you ask of them?

- *Call you out when needed.* Over many years of rehearsals, I've heard it all from my posse. "That doesn't sound like you," Lisa said, with an ear that knows when I'm inauthentic. "You're coming across as a pompous ass," Hilary noted, hip to my occasional runaway ego. It hurts to hear, but they propel me out of a sense of pride and a competitive spirit to do better, rise higher as a thinker and orator.

- *Ask for honesty and be willing to accept it when it comes.* You're not going to get honest feedback unless you solicit it, respect the time of those who are willing to offer it, and perhaps most important, take it into consideration. No one wants to give advice to someone who is chronically dismissive of it. Why bother? If you want someone to give it to you straight, you must make the space for that to happen. This means not resenting the person afterward, or you will never get the truth from them again. You can't punish colleagues, especially those who work for you, for offering you an honest assessment of your actions or words. If you receive tough but fair feedback, or resistance to one of your ideas, you can't change the relationship. This is hard because we're human; no one likes to be criticized. You have the power to establish trust around honest feedback.

- *Review your work in draft.* Find a friend who is not beholden to you to read your work in draft. I'm not talking about a sub-ordinate or consultant, but a true pal who will speak truth to you. For me, no one has more standing or a truer heart when it comes to critiquing my work than my wife, Robin. She is my ultimate reader and editor. Over years of working on various books—a memoir that made little sense, an unreadable novel (both of which are abandoned in my bottom desk drawer), and now this book, she has been the most loyal and candid reviewer. I always approach her with a bit of pleading, "Do you have time to read a chapter?" She will agree and receive my pages. She then sets them aside until she has the time and frame of mind to give my work her undivided attention. I know my job is to wait. Not whine. Not beg. More often than not, she returns my pages, with her chicken-scratched handwritten notes in the margin—bits of encouragement sandwiched between notations to "be funnier," or "needs to be more original," and always the admonishment to "keep going,

I know you can do better." Those words keep me humble but also spur me on.

- *Acceptance is key.* Yes, the initial and natural response to criticism is to reject it. Fight this urge. I did not throw my friend on the beach into the waves when she told me she didn't want to get the vaccine. I stopped and listened. Likewise, if I receive criticism about a communications strategy, or an idea is shot down or met with resistance, I take it. I let it settle into my mind. I marinate on the counterpoints offered. I may end up disagreeing with all or part of a criticism, but only after I have thought it through. This is the ultimate humility. Don't react by automatically rejecting input or getting defensive. Take a breath and count to ten before saying anything. Ask questions to understand more about what the criticism is about. Ultimately, we all must arrive at our own conclusions to pursue a course of communications or change direction, or not. But if you take the time to really consider the pros and cons of others, that humility will have a positive effect on what you produce.

- *Act on it.* Finally, if you want people to feel that it was worth being honest with you, show them that you've incorporated their words into your actions. No, this does not have to be consistent. Not all feedback is right or useful. But at least show that you respected it by accepting it gracefully and considering it. If you received good advice, take it.

Ultimately, humility is a self-confident expression of admiration of (even love for) people. When communication is rooted in humility, it is an act of respect that pays homage to those we admire. In November of 2018, I created a LinkedIn series called #YouDo to recognize women I deeply respect. I was reacting to the #MeToo movement. At that time, the hashtag had gone viral, as the world woke up to the extent of sexual harassment and violence in our culture. It was an extraordinarily important awakening to a devastating reality many women and some men face. It was also very sad. Without taking anything away from that crucial unveiling, I wanted to flip the coin; rather than point a finger at perpetrators, I'd shine a light on role models.

Each day for a month, I posted a photograph and brief introduction of a different woman from a range of disciplines. I introduced the concept by saying that I wanted to express my gratitude to the women who have inspired me. The debut profile was Sue Desmond-Hellmann, MD, MPH, and then-CEO of the Bill & Melinda Gates Foundation, whom I applauded for helping to eradicate illness around the world, for celebrating science, for her amazing achievement in biotech, higher education, and philanthropy. Sue reminds us that we are not one thing, but many. That our reach is deep and broad. Luckily for me, two years later Sue joined the Pfizer board of directors.

My "You Do" hashtag grew in popularity. Some of the most-liked posts included Reshma Saujani, founder and CEO of Girls Who Code; Mellody Hobson, president of Ariel Capital; and the late Madeleine Albright, former US secretary of state. This project brought me so much joy and wonderful responses from the women I honored and their followers. Simple, humble, truthful expressions pave the pathway toward the most meaningful and memorable communications.

CHAPTER EIGHT

Lighten Up!

Delight with Humor

"I'LL GIVE YOU TWO COWS FOR HER," THE ELDERLY MAN said, pointing his knotty wood walking stick in my direction.

Wait. What? Was he really making an offer to trade a couple of his skinny bovines for me? Yes, he was.

It was 2013. I was leading a small group of Pfizer colleagues to see our philanthropic work in maternal clinics in the United Republic of Tanzania, an East African country known for its vast expanses of wilderness. We had arrived by van that morning at the medical outpost to tour the small treatment rooms. It was afternoon now, and hot. We were sitting with some of the local leaders right outside the clinic in the scant shade, trading pleasantries. As we wrapped up the meeting, an elderly man appeared seemingly out of nowhere—a shock of tightly cropped white hair framing his thin face, his smile a row of uneven teeth, his body draped in a brightly colored cloak—to make his bold proposition. He was quite serious. The air tingled with tension. My Western hackles went up.

I'm a woman, not a chattel, I thought. I was also nearly 7,500 miles from New York City and didn't want to incite an international incident. But I would not be thought of as or traded like a commodity. I was angry and offended and speechless—and unfortunately, it probably showed all over my face. In my line of work, I should have an impenetrable poker face, but I don't. I was scrambling for the appropriate reply to this degrading insult. What were the right words to express my disgust and disdain? Everyone seemed shocked. As the head of our delegation, I thought it was incumbent on me to respond.

Then I saw Albert stepping forward. At that time, he was not yet Pfizer's CEO or my boss. He was a fellow executive whom I was still getting to know. He'd been quiet on the trip, so I couldn't imagine what he was going to say. Albert went right up to the man, looked him square in the eye, and said, "This woman will not be sold . . . for less than four cows!"

Oh. I got it. Good thing I kept my mouth shut. Back in the states, I could have knocked a guy who said this on his noggin, but here, in East Africa, I was being paid a compliment and needed a sense of humor to see it. No, I was not in Kansas anymore, and I'd better lighten up.

Those assembled were momentarily silent as they took in Albert's retort. And, then we all began to smile. Giggles rolled into belly laughs. Albert had diffused the moment with humor. Levity was the antidote to the awkwardness. That afternoon in a dusty Tanzanian village was the first, but not the last time I saw Albert win the day with his ability to use humor effectively, to not take a situation or himself too seriously. It's a way that he and many other powerful communicators express themselves during stressful times. I'm not suggesting a stand-up routine or delivering funny jokes. I can't tell a joke to save my life. I'm talking about something subtler—playfulness or lightheartedness that highlights our humanity but does not disparage it. Happiness and joy turn potentially sticky situations into memorable positive stories, ones that are fun to repeat. Albert and I love to recall the "cow story." We laugh every time.

While dedicating a chapter to humor may seem trivial, it isn't, because humor, used correctly, is a truly brilliant, winning communications technique. So much of my ambition for this book is to help you, kind reader, build the skills to move hearts in ways that make lasting change. That's important work, a serious life-altering endeavor, and humor can help. Ed Catmull is a computer scientist who, in 1974, titled his senior thesis at the University of Utah School of Computing, "A Subdivision Algorithm for Computer Display of Curved Surfaces." That makes him a serious dude. Ed went on to cofound of Pixar and become president of Walt Disney and Pixar Animation Studios. Not long ago he wrote, "A sense of humor is part of what makes us human. It's a deeply connecting and empowering piece. Deploying humor doesn't make light of serious things, it means you're able to move forward despite those serious things. . . . Where there is serious work punctuated by levity—that's where we find meaning."[1]

Humor is also a leadership power tool. Jennifer Aaker and Naomi Bagdonas, authors of the book *Humor, Seriously: Why Humor Is a Secret Weapon in Business and Life*, are also creators and teachers of a course called "Humor: Serious Business" at Stanford's Graduate School of Business. They claim to "teach some of the world's most ambitious, smart, and caffeine-addled business minds on how to use humor and levity to transform their future organizations and lives."

In the Stanford Business School *Think Fast, Talk Smart* podcast that aired in June 2020, Bagdonas said, "It used to be that leaders needed to be revered. And now they need to be understood. And all the while, humor is a particularly potent elixir for trust." She further explains, "And when we laugh with someone . . . our brains release a hormone called oxytocin, and we're essentially cued to form an emotional bond with that person. And oxytocin, by the way, is the same hormone that's released during sex and childbirth, fun fact."

If that course had been offered when I was contemplating graduate school, I might have signed up for it. I have observed in multiple business, political, and civic settings the role humor plays helping to articulate a path forward even through the dark woods of hostility, boredom, or apathy. I've been amazed the way humor, appropriately employed, can help communicate tough feedback, beat back corporate bureaucracy, or clear out competitive clutter to let your idea or product shine through.

Humor for Achieving Workplace Harmony

In 2010, my department received low scores on a culture survey. According to the report, my division was stymied by an array of unhelpful workplace behaviors ranging from unclear expectations to fear of retaliation for mistakes. I knew it was incumbent on me to share those poor findings with the team and have some straight talk about what we needed to do together to improve the morale. I invited everyone to a town hall, but I was stumped as to how to set the right stage for a candid, meaningful, and different conversation. I didn't want to convey any defensiveness or insecurity. Workplace harmony is important to me, and I was ready to dive in to address the shortcomings.

Then it hit me when I was watching a rerun of *The Devil Wears Prada*. During the opening scene, the main character, a high-powered fashion editor named Miranda Priestly (played brilliantly by Meryl Streep) arrives at work. The entire staff is in a frenzy, preparing her coffee just so, arranging her papers just as she likes them on her desk, and mostly, getting out of her way. The staff feared her. Miranda comes into the office, throws her coat and bag on the receptionist's desk, and begins shouting at the staff. She's cast a pall over the place. It's funny, but also a sad scene that plays out across too many offices. I reeled up a clip of that vignette from the movie as an icebreaker to our conversation; the tension melted from the room, shoulders unhitched, and we could begin the job of having a game-changing conversation about how we could all contribute to a more relaxed and productive environment.

Here are some of the breakthrough outcomes you can achieve through humor and levity.

Easing isolation. Growing up in the suburbs, I quickly learned that all those houses tucked neatly together in rows of subdivisions didn't necessarily represent feelings of companionship or community. Even in the most picturesque neighborhoods, there are lonely folks behind those picket fences. At least that was my experience when I was growing up and what drove me to read Erma Bombeck's column in the *St. Louis Post-Dispatch*. Bombeck, the self-described "former obituary writer and homeroom mother," wrote humorously on suburban life. Even though I was just a kid, I related to her. I chuckled over her funny lines as I read the paper at the kitchen table. Bombeck offered solace to all of us who felt trapped in suburbia.

In her bestseller, *The Grass Is Always Greener Over the Septic Tank*, Bombeck reports on the migration of 30 million settlers to the suburbs following World War II. In the opening chapter, "Station Wagons . . . Ho!," she writes, "The selling of the suburbs made the coronation of Queen Elizabeth look like an impulse." Of course, the men and women who built lives in the suburbs were recovering from both a devastating Great Depression and the horrors of war; maintaining a perfect lawn and other domestic activities were reassuring forms of therapy for many of them. But the suburbs had also taken a social toll on people as the 1950s progressed into the 1960s.

That's when Bombeck hit her stride, which allowed her to make fun of the suburban myths: "The suburbs didn't invent sex—it only gave it wider distribution." She chided men for their obsession with their lawns: "Every casual greeting opens with: How's the lawn, Buddy?" She poked fun at our traditions: "Halloween was my sixteenth favorite holiday. It rated somewhere between the April 15th tax deadline and

New Year's Eve without a babysitter." She lampooned our daily hab-its: "In 1946, the suburbs suffered its first plague. It struck with little warning and attacked the weak, the bored, the vulnerable seeking re-lief from the monotony. Its name was television and by 1966, it would enslave 62 million families." This was my life she was poking fun at, and I laughed along with the jokes.

The place Bombeck wrote about, a neighborhood called Subur-bian Gems, was real, as were most of the characters in her book. She wrote, "Certainly, the frustrations, the loneliness, the laughter, the challenges, and especially the analogy were for real. We were like pi-oneers, in a sense, leaving what we knew in search of our American dream." Like the best humorists, Bombeck touched us because she wrote about the things we recognized and understood. She knew us. Got us. Teased and cared for us. Shared our vision for ourselves. Made our loads a little lighter, our isolation less acute. Her communications advice stands the test of time: "Hook 'em with the lead. Hold 'em with laughter. Exit with a quip they won't forget."[2] The proof of Bombeck's winning formula was that her column, "At Wit's End," was syndicated throughout the world in 542 newspapers. There is a reason why the Erma Bombeck Writing Competition and Writers' Workshop both continue to be offered today and attract twenty-first-century comedy superstars—her subject matter, style, and techniques remain relevant.[3]

I try to channel her sharp, inventive style and self-deprecation whenever I have the chance, because the workplace can be a lonely en-vironment, too. Employees rush in and barrel out to make their com-muter trains. Lunches are scarfed down at the desk. Postpandemic, working from home has not helped the desire or ability to build tight-knit teams. Whenever I can, I try to inject a little Bombeckian humor into my written and spoken communications, because relat-able humor creates connections and builds bridges of recognition and understanding that we're all in the same boat. Let's sail in it together.

Light, good-natured humor in a business or professional setting can also be just enough to keep the humanity flowing and the arrogance at bay. In terms of business communications, humor, when done right, brings people together around an issue or cause simply by helping break the ice, diffuse tense situations, boost morale, build trust, and encourage creativity.

Creating community. Our twenties and thirties are prime years to build relationships and expand our professional networks. It's never been easy to create meaningful connections, and Covid has made it harder. Some have managed to create relationships online or in socially distanced settings, while others have, sadly, languished in current conditions.

I was impressed to see how a member of my extended family, Ella Weil, found a way to break into a new city and safely find like-minded friends via her love of comedy and creative use of her eighty-square-foot backyard. Ella, twenty-nine, and her significant other, Kyle Kallman, moved to Los Angeles to pursue their professional dreams. She wanted to do stand-up comedy, and Kyle had an eye trained on writing. They knew no one. But they were fortunate to find a place in Los Angeles within walking distance of The Comedy Store and The Laugh Factory. When the Covid-19 virus pushed them outdoors, Ella and Kyle started a comedy club behind their house. Named for the street where they lived, the Dicks Street Show was born and comes to life the third Friday of every month. The stage is a small riser created of wood spray-painted blue. They string the area with café lights and surround it with fifty rented metal folding chairs. For $12, show-goers get six or so stand-up performances and all the beer and wine they can enjoy. "Each month the audience gets a little bigger and the show more legit," Ella explained.

"It's the ultimate form of entertainment because the shared experience of laughing together is something people value very highly," Ella continued. The comedians cover issues of wealth, class, lifestyle, relationships, dating, and sex, to name only a few. "People like to come because we are tackling deep topics in an accessible way." Creating the conditions whereby touchy subjects can be considered in new ways is the magic of humor. Enjoying that recalibration and reflection in communal settings is icing on the cake. If you happen to find yourself in Los Angeles on the third Friday of the month, you may want to drop by the Dicks Street Show and meet some lovely young people.

Removing the shame. In the summer of 2017, I sent out an unusual invitation to my corporate affairs team. It read, "In life, mistakes happen. What's important is learning from them and, on occasion, looking back and having a good laugh about them!"

> Join for our first ever "My Blooper Reel" open mic night, where corporate affairs colleagues can share some of their funniest and most embarrassing work stories, lessons learned, and words of wisdom. Whether it be a mistake that you were certain would be a career-ender, a time that you planned perfectly but went horrifically wrong anyway, or the most outrageous advice you received from a coworker, we want to hear it all. The good, the bad, and the ugly. Come with your most outlandish story!

In preparation, we decorated the company auditorium with a single microphone, a bar stool, and a brick-wall image on the screen to give the impression of a comedy club. We made clear that we were creating a safe space where we could admit mistakes without repercussion. On the day of the event, people not only showed up but arrived early, so excited were they to have their turn at stand-up comedy—with the joke being on themselves. I kicked off with the story I told earlier in this book about my terrible mistake of sharing my boss's confidential news about his retirement and creating an embarrassing news leak. I told the story in great detail, revealed the most traumatizing elements, and laced it with laugh lines. The crowd chuckled along with me. I wrapped up my short set with the reflection that my mistake—like most—taught me an important life lesson. From that experience forward, I have never broken a confidence.

As I walked off, my teammates hopped on stage one after another and, with extraordinary self-deprecation and witticism, shared their most awkward mistakes. Top-secret papers left on the subway and highly confidential emails sent to the wrong recipients were just two of the many heart-stopping errors that my colleagues revealed humorously. They hammed it up, and we laughed it off. It was healing and helpful, as we saw how we could learn from one another and build our resilience. Humor also showed us that we can recover from the great majority of mistakes we make in life and in business.

Selling stuff. Cliff Freeman was an advertising legend who passed away in the fall of 2021 at age eighty. I didn't know Mr. Freeman personally, but we all know his work. Freeman's obituary in the *Wall Street Journal* ran under the headline, "Cliff Freeman Sold Burgers and Pizzas with Wacky Ads." The piece noted, "He was most famous for dreaming up the 'Where's the beef?' ad, mocking a competitor of the Wendy's fast-food chain in the mid-1980s and creating a phrase still echoing in the national conversation 35 years later." I first heard the line when I was in college, but I never forgot it.

One of Freeman's competitors, Keith Reinhard, chairman emeritus of DDB Worldwide, who worked for McDonald's when Freeman was working for Wendy's, remembered: "What he demonstrated was that slapstick, bizarre humor, and wild exaggeration not only can cut through the clutter but also create massive good-will for a brand and lift sales."

The irreverent burger line wasn't Freeman's only hit. He also came up with the unforgettable jingle for Almond Joy candy bar: "Sometimes you feel like a nut. Sometimes you don't." It was silly, happy, and ultimately, memorable.

And speaking of "nuts," another one of my favorite examples of poking fun at oneself was the campaign led by the New York Committee in the Public Interest in 1976 in the run-up to the city hosting the Democratic National Convention. The advertising firm Ogilvy & Mather came up with a "crazy" idea for a campaign that appeared on subways, buses, and in newspapers. Rumor is that it was inspired by a quote from the colorful New York congresswoman Bella Abzug, but it's never been fully confirmed. The tagline was, "You have to be a little crazy to live in New York, but you'd be nuts to live anywhere else."

I've seen many destinations tout their beautiful beaches or dramatic skylines, but this was the first time I saw a place make fun of itself and laugh at its own peculiar psychology. It spoke directly to the mindset that convinced me to leave the Midwest and come to the Big Apple. Whether you are selling hamburgers, candy bars, or big cities, a relevant laugh line that recognizes the ideas that bind us together can boost the bottom line.

A Humorist Walks into a Minefield

Humor is not without its risks and downsides, especially in our woke world. To do it right, you must be mindful, kind, and thoughtful. But does it have a place in the modern corporation? Can it fit in? For sure.

A series of studies have consistently showed that humor has a positive impact in the workplace. It reduces stress and enhances your intake of oxygen-rich air, increasing your brain's release of endorphins. Laughter can boost productivity. In one study, researchers found that after watching a comedy clip, employees were 10 percent more productive than those who were not exposed to the clip. Another study found that using humor at work and in communications can make people and companies seem more competent, as long as said humor is within the bounds of decency. So, while there are risks, the benefits of humor far outweigh them.[4] Here are some suggestions to avoid the quicksand.

Challenge familiar conventions. One way to get people to reconsider orthodox notions is through humor, especially if you use familiar concepts everyone relates to. When they see the humor in the idiocy or irrelevance of certain conventions, we can change them. *New Yorker* cartoonist Liza Donnelly gave a TED Talk titled, "Drawing on Humor for Change" in 2020 that's been viewed nearly 1.5 million times. The audience laughs their way through her seven-minute presentation as the points of her story are illuminated by her wonderful cartoons. And yet her message is dead serious. She talks about how women can change the rules that govern their lives.

Donnelly says that women plus humor can equal change, demonstrated by collaborating with cartoonists from around the world. Each culture has its own rules that impact women, Donnelly explains, but the rules are universal in their result, which is to constrain women socially, economically, or politically. The power of cartoons (and humor in general) allows us to get at the truth quickly and succinctly but in a nonthreatening way, reaching both the intellect and the heart. Donnelly explains, "We have the great potential to be change agents and we can make change one laugh at a time." She argues that we can confront and transform accepted codes of behavior that don't work for us through humor, which is far less threatening and much more engaging than turgid lectures on progressive talking points. In other words, you not only get more flies with honey, but also get more flies with honey that has a relatable punchline.

Relieve the tension. In 2009, when newly elected President Barack Obama was rolling out his roster of diplomatic envoys, he was met with a barrage of criticism for selecting from his Rolodex of old friends and prodigious fundraisers. This political patronage practice is not new and is often the subject of rebuke and ridicule. In the case of President Obama, expectations were high that things would be different this time. He had run on a campaign of political reform and made promises that he wouldn't place noncareer diplomats in foreign posts. But, alas, the first of President Obama's ambassadors was not drawn from the professional ranks but the old boys' network.

Among his earliest appointments was Phil Murphy to be ambassador to Germany. Murphy was a twenty-three-year veteran of Goldman Sachs, where he held several high-ranking positions and accumulated considerable wealth. Also among those named in the first wave was Charles Rivkin, who was slated to be ambassador to France. Rivkin had been the CEO of several entertainment companies, including WildBrain, and the former head of the Jim Henson Company. Another one out of the nominations gate was Louis Susman to be ambassador to the Court of Saint James in the United Kingdom. He was the recently retired vice chairman of Citigroup Global Markets (and my dad). For each of these high-profile nominations, their backgrounds and roles as commercial players and fundraisers fueled questions about their qualifications and worthiness. Obama appeared to have failed his own test.

The president came under fire. "It's time to end the spoils system and to stop renting out these ambassadorships for fabulous sums of money," said Susan Johnson, president of the American Foreign Service Association, which monitors nominations.[5] As the commentary grew critical, I worried for my dad. "The internet is blowing up with complaints," I told him. Neither he nor I knew exactly what to do. We were in the uncharted waters of the political nominations process and gagged by the requirement that the nominee remain silent during the period. Still, I tried to keep a close eye on things for my dad.

Then one day, White House press secretary Robert Gibbs was at the podium taking questions from the media on a range of subjects when the question of political appointment to diplomatic posts came up. I took a swift inhale and then held my breath. What would Press Secretary Gibbs say to defend the president's choices? Would he dodge the inquiry or extol their virtues? Would he stick up for how experienced and talented a guy my dad is, and the others are too? Nope. Gibbs did something much savvier. He smiled and took a more comedic approach. First, he warmed up by mentioning that Charlie Rivkin was, among other things, fluent in French. And then, in total deadpan he noted, that Louis Susman is qualified "because . . . he speaks English." Chuckles rippled across the press corps.

With that witty comment, Gibbs burst the bubble of those who sought to make an issue out of my father's accomplishments (which, by the way, are many). The question of his readiness and qualifications to serve was rarely raised from that day forward. In this case, humor had won the day. As I've seen many times, a playful or lighthearted response can be enormously effective.

By the way, I feel obligated to add that these ambassadors went on to serve with distinction throughout President Obama's term. They represented our country with dignity and vigor. Today, former ambassador Murphy is the governor of New Jersey, former ambassador Rivkin is the chairman of the Motion Picture Association, and my dad is, well, retired and continues to offer his superb advice and counsel to many politicians and other business leaders (with special discounted rates for my brother and me).

Skip the sarcasm. Sarcasm is a form of humor that uses irony to mock or convey contempt. It's often wry and biting. It's OK for the comedy club, but really has no place in the office. My second boss on Capitol Hill, Senator Fritz Hollings of South Carolina, was very smart and amusing but on occasion, his humor drifted into sarcasm, and then it wasn't funny anymore. In 1981, there was a heated debate on the Senate floor over legislation supporting voluntary prayer in the public schools. Senator Hollings was speaking in support of the measure when several senators including Senator Howard Metzenbaum of Ohio interrupted Hollings and tried to challenge him.

Hollings fired back and said, "The questioning will now be done by the senator from B'nai B'rith," which was interpreted by many as a slur on Metzenbaum's Jewish faith. It probably was. Hollings later apologized to Metzenbaum, and the comment was stricken from the record. But the damage was done. The taint of anti-Semitism hung over Hollings from that day. Sarcasm is an easy pothole to tumble into, especially when one has a quick mind and a sharp tongue. I often find myself swallowing a comment that I think is witty but borders on sarcasm. A laugh isn't worth the price I'll pay for a sniping quip. As my friend Dana Perino wrote, "Sarcasm is like cheap wine—it leaves a terrible aftertaste."[6]

This next point should go without saying, but I'll make it anyway: absolutely anything that may be construed as racist, sexist, ageist, or ableist, or hits on cultural sensitivities can and will damage your standing in your community or company, and can hurt professional relationships of all kinds, with employees, customers, and clients. There is no place for it. Even if an individual is not personally offended by off-color humor, they could very well find it an unwelcome and unprofessional breaking of rules, which is just as bad. Never employ humor at the expense of someone else.

Don't be the court jester. I learned at an early age how to entertain. After dinners at my grandparents' house, my family encouraged (expected) the grandchildren to perform a skit. We were a playhouse of six actors. I was the oldest and the only girl, so many of our productions had a *Snow White and the Seven Dwarfs* feel to them. I loved the attention and the spotlight, maybe a bit too much. I carried this desire to please and perform from my youth into adulthood. I often bring a toast or a roast, or I harangue a colleague to join me in a skit for festive business occasions like a recent retirement dinner for a team member. I hope to add some warmth, good humor, and memorability. I think people count on me to offer these bon mots. A company's chief communicator commonly plays a prominent role in creating company merriment. In these moments, I take care (and sometimes fail) not to overstep the mark. The line between having fun and being foolish is dangerously fine.

Do not allow your good intentions to tip you over into the category of court jester. Originally, royal courts in English history employed a jester to tell stories, play music, and perform acrobatics. In *King Lear*, the court jester offers insights and warnings to the monarch. The jester's ability to speak freely and frankly because of his low position stands in contrast to senior members of court, who are afraid to approach the king. Through Shakespeare's work, the jester or fool is usually a clever commoner who uses his wit to outdo people of higher social standing. In modern terms, the jester is seen more as a buffoon seeking attention through inappropriate behavior or ridiculous acts. Avoid the trap of becoming a carnival barker or other vulgar characters.

Beware of the office party. Be particularly careful at office parties. I love to dance, and when the DJ starts to spin tunes, I'm usually the first one on the dance floor. I try to keep myself in check, as being a breakthrough communicator doesn't mean I need to break dance or be the one with the lampshade on my head at the end of the evening. I also watch myself at open bars. You want to be sure people are laughing with you and not at you.

True Confessions of a Joy Struggler

In early 2019, Pfizer was updating its corporate values. We knew that if we wrote too many, or if they were clichéd, employees would dismiss them as propaganda on poster board. We were seeking a few, meaningful, high-impact concepts.

Albert Bourla, a few other executive leadership team members, and I gathered several times to discuss these. We tossed ideas around. The first value that spoke to us was *courage*. We would need boldness to achieve our purpose. The second was *excellence*, which is essential when running a global business of our scale. The third, *equity*, was progressive for a pharmaceutical company and necessary, given that human health is our work. Would we be happy with these three? We considered it.

"There's something missing," Albert said. "Should we add *happiness*?"

"How about *joy*?" I said in nearly a whisper. It felt explosive to suggest something so emotional, so human. Joy is a close cousin to humor, and the element that keeps humor from going off the rails into insult and injury.

We looked at one another and knew that we had hit paydirt. Joy defined our aspiration for the fun, happy culture we craved. I skipped home that evening with Beethoven's "Ode to Joy" blaring through my earbuds, waving my arms as I pretended to conduct the symphonic piece.

In the days that followed we added a vivid description and behaviors that underpinned each value. For *joy*, we wrote our intention was to: "(1) Take pride: We celebrate our impact because our work changes lives; (2) Recognize one another: We honor our colleagues and their efforts because praise sparks passion; and (3) Have fun: We can always make room to be playful because laughter is good medicine too."

I felt ownership of this work and took enormous pleasure watching people's faces light up when they heard that joy had made the list. We had nailed it.

So, imagine how devastated I was when, two years later, I received my colleagues' feedback and found I had terrible scores on the joy metrics. Not just low, not merely below average, but rock-bottom-of-the-barrel results to questions, including whether I "create a positive atmosphere" or "create opportunities for fun." I failed to embody the spirit of the value. Apparently, it was unanimous that I am a stick-in-the-mud.

Once I got over feeling shocked and ashamed, I dusted myself off and committed to being better, and not just on my scores but on living the value of joy. But how?

First, I had to understand my problem and took some time to reflect. I had to admit that I'm uncomfortable with a lot of what I see as corporate-mandated merriment: stickers to celebrate achievements feel trivial, goofy team-building exercises feel inauthentic, and surprise parties make me anxious. I worried I didn't have the joy gene or maybe I'd just grown cranky with age.

I struggled with needing to digest the company's joy value and make it my own. I thought about what gives me joy. I love nothing more than long walks, reading, and intimate conversation. Those activities may not sound snappy, but they make me happy. I realized that they are the roots from which I can authentically express joy. Some of the happiest times we've had as a team were when I tapped into these interests.

As a devoted walker, I always plan a leisurely hike with the team. We've had a hitch when one teammate hit her head on a low-lying branch and another grumbled at the start about the "forced march," but these walks have created many good connections as we stroll and share thoughts along the path. It's a form of joy.

To make the point that joy matters, we end each of my team town halls with short films expressing happiness. We've seen one colleague riding a surfboard, another sharing a traditional Indian dance, and a father introducing us to his newborn daughter.

I realized that even though I can't tell a joke or be overtly funny, I can still be lighthearted and playful. These moments of joy have drawn our team closer together, opened us to our differences and similarities, and form the bedrock of our ability to relate to one another and communicate with creativity and impact.

CHAPTER NINE

Look for Answers in the Rearview Mirror

Reflect and Honor

IN JULY OF 2020, FIVE LONG MONTHS BEFORE PFIZER KNEW whether its vaccine would effectively provide protection against Covid-19, I reached out to National Geographic (NatGeo), a division of the Walt Disney Company, to discuss a collaboration on a documentary film about Pfizer's all-hands-on-deck effort to find an effective vaccine in record time.

NatGeo was the obvious and best media outlet for this project because it has both scientific credibility and journalistic integrity. The NatGeo team responded to the idea with enthusiasm, and the project came together very quickly, without the usual haggling over parameters, access, timelines, and so on. The network understood that it would gain rare behind-the-scenes access to the largest pharmaceutical company in the world as it pursued the development, manufacturing, and distribution of a desperately needed vaccine in response to a global health emergency. NatGeo needed Pfizer's cooperation to make this movie.

And I needed NatGeo.

Why? Because I believed that during this unprecedented drive for the vaccine, my role included a responsibility to be Pfizer's documentarian. There are lessons that future Pfizer scientists, researchers, and executives, including those on future communication teams, would learn and use. I enjoy playing the part of company archivist, and I am also humbled by it. It's a big responsibility, one that isn't official and doesn't show up in my job description or year-end assessment (or my résumé). Yet it's one aspect of my job that I most love and appreciate. Legacy and institutional memory are essential ingredients of effective communications. We cannot speak on behalf of an idea, a company, or a brand if we don't know its roots and heritage. "Once upon a time . . . " begins many children's tales and oral histories for a reason. Reflection is the ideal starting point for beginning a story, even if the memories themselves are not included in the final draft—history helps you get there. Moreover, sharing both the challenges and victories with our teams and leaving them behind as a legacy of learning for the future is a form of continuity. It helps establish consistency, which in turn makes communicating about it stronger and more assured.

In the case of the Covid-19 vaccine, I also wanted to record our actions and make this documentary for a guy named Charlie. That would be Charles Pfizer, the German chemist who, in 1849, founded Charles Pfizer & Company in Brooklyn, New York. Charles Pfizer and his cousin Charles Erhart started a fine-chemicals business with a $2,500 loan from Charlie's father (with Pfizer's market cap over $200 billion today, that would be one of the better investments made from the Bank of Dad).

Pfizer (the man) and Erhart had immediate success with their first product, a flavorful form of santonin—a drug used to treat intestinal worms, a common affliction in the mid-1800s. The subsequent demand for disinfectants, preservatives, and painkillers during the American Civil War doubled the company's revenues and fostered its expansion. In the late 1800s, its citric acid production soared with the increasing popularity of cola drinks, producing decades of growth for the company. During World War II, when the US and UK governments approached the largest pharmaceutical and chemical companies to enlist them in the race to mass-produce penicillin, Pfizer succeeded in producing the largest quantity of the new "wonder drug."

Now, nearly eighty years later, here Pfizer was again, potentially making medical and societal history. I had better capture what just might be the latest chapter in a great American success story.

Not only was this story relevant for the history books, but also for the more than 80,000 people who worked at Pfizer. They deserved a tangible commemoration of their efforts. For many of us, this would be *the* story we would tell for the rest of our lives. If successful, it would be a proud tale we would share with our children and grandchildren. Heck, we would tell anyone who would listen. If it wasn't successful, well, there would still be valuable lessons learned. I agree with the immortal words of Winston Churchill, "Those that fail to learn from history are doomed to repeat it."

NatGeo swung into action and hired a production firm, The Documentary Group, to make the film. The combined NatGeo and Documentary Group team made clear that they were not interested in a long-form feature film that would be an advertisement for Pfizer. This would not, and could not, be an exercise in corporate vanity or a puff piece. Viewers would see right through anything less than a thoroughly researched, investigative film. Otherwise we would risk being deservedly mocked.

The NatGeo directors handed me a list of Pfizer executives to interview for the film. Naturally, Albert Bourla was on the list, along with the head of manufacturing, the top vaccine scientist, and many more key players. I worried about taking time away from these executives' more pressing duties to prepare for and then sit in front of the cameras for questioning. In moviemaking, long hours of filming are required to yield a few minutes of tape that make it into final production.

The director also wanted access to film in the labs and the plants. These essential facilities were tightly secured during Covid. I began to panic. Was I giving a full-access pass to people with cameras rolling? What if we failed? What if our vaccine didn't work? What if we had squandered valuable time and money? And I was the one with the big idea to televise a potential debacle.

During the early fall of 2020, The Documentary Group made multiple trips to our laboratories in Pearl River, New York, and to our manufacturing plant in Kalamazoo, Michigan. It shot footage of the labs, the vaccine production, and distribution capabilities. The crew filmed interviews with all the key players, managing to adhere to all safety and Covid-related protocols. I thought we were done. But then, the filmmakers requested even more time with the CEO and other Pfizer leaders. In the end, they interviewed Albert several times over many hours, as the director chose his Greek-accented, baritone voice to narrate the film. It was an inspired call, but I worried that patience of Albert and our top leaders was running thin. My stress level was through the roof.

Later that fall, the production team began to press me for access to film the readout when we learned whether or not our vaccine was effective. Specifically, they wanted to train their cameras on our faces at the very fateful moment when we would receive the call from our scientists with the news from the Data and Safety Monitoring Board (DSMB), an independent committee of research experts, physicians, and patient advocates who monitor the progress of a clinical trial for safety and effectiveness data. Its findings would determine our success or failure. My feeling, at this point, was that I had gone too far to pull back. "OK," I said, sounding shaky.

Then we learned that the critical board would meet to review the data from our Covid-19 clinical trials on Sunday morning, November 8.

Albert gathered a few of us in a conference room in our offices in Cos Cob, Connecticut, to hear the news.

Albert; Mikael Dolsten, our chief scientist; General Counsel Doug Lankler; Yolanda Lyle, Albert's chief of staff; and I were there. We tried to kill time until the phone call came that would deliver our vaccine's fate. We watched the Sunday morning news shows on the office television and drank too much coffee. Yolanda busied herself attending to company administration, and Mikael checked in with his wife who had recovered from Covid. I binged on KIND bars in the office pantry, while Doug tried to amuse and distract Albert with light banter.

Finally, Yolanda received a text that the results were in. We gathered around the conference table. I looked out the window at the fall foliage and knew that our view of ourselves would never be the same. This was an epic inflection point that would lead to success or failure.

Through a speakerphone, our scientist Bill Gruber said, "We have good news . . ." The cameras were rolling. Bill reported that the DSMB recommended that Pfizer move immediately to gain emergency use authorization of our vaccine. Our chief scientist said, "Oh my God, this is the greatest medical advance in a century!"

Despite social distance guidelines, we hugged. Doug fist-pumped the air; I did a little impromptu dance. Our explosion of joy was caught on film. That instant reflected our dreams realized and hope for an anxious world. It became the anchor scene of the film that aired on March 11, 2021, one year to the day that the World Health Organization declared the pandemic. (The film, *Mission Possible: The Race for a Vaccine*, is available on YouTube.)

I'm proud of the film and consider it the greatest gift I could give to Pfizer and my colleagues around the world. Research conducted by the Disney Company measured the impact of the documentary on both the Pfizer brand and overall vaccine sentiments. Its findings included higher trust levels for Pfizer (from 66 percent to 83 percent of adults surveyed) and a greater inclination of viewers to get the Covid-19 vaccine after viewing the film. The responses from colleagues, friends, and even competitors to the film were even more gratifying and it proved that making *Mission Possible* was a risk worth taking.[1]

Caught on Film

While *Mission Possible* was successful, garnering more than 21 million viewers, not all such efforts turn out so well. The outcome of embedding film crews to record history doesn't always yield a positive outcome—and maybe it shouldn't if your interest is in authentically documenting a moment in time. Sometimes the results are painful, but the act of documenting history can still be a noble cause and a chance to gain insights for future endeavors, so is often worth the risks involved.

Unfortunately, for Christine Quinn, the popular, outspoken speaker of the New York City Council who ran for mayor of the city in 2013, the decision to allow the *New York Times* to video behind the scenes was regrettable. Most people thought she was a shoo-in at the start of her run. Chris was a dynamic speaker (New York's second most powerful post after mayor) with a well-defined social and economic plan that would help middle-class New Yorkers. Chris's poll numbers were high, and she appeared to relish campaigning. As a result, she began to build on her front-runner status.

I've known Chris for years, but was still flattered when she called and asked, "Will you be my finance chair?" Learning from my father's history as a top political fundraiser, I understood my job was to ensure she had the campaign funds to carry her through the race. I loved the thought of being involved in a citywide campaign and spending time with a woman I admired on a platform I believed in. "Sure," I replied, taking on this volunteer role without hesitation.

Chris and her team were confident she would win. Maybe we were all overconfident. When the *New York Times* reached out and negotiated with the campaign manager to embed a camera within the campaign, we agreed to it. I was excited by the prospect, pleased that an important international news organization would be documenting this historic mayoral race, when a woman and a member of the LGBTQ+ community would be elected mayor to arguably the nation's most important city for the first time.

In the early scenes of the film, we hear Chris say, "Blast it," referring to Bruce Springsteen's "Born to Run," which pumped through her campaign van's speakers. She and her wife, Kim, sing along. Over the course of the thirty-minute film, those initial ebullient moments showing Chris shaking hands with sympathetic voters, speaking before large crowds, and embracing Kim give way to images of hostile protestors chanting, "A, B, C: Anybody but Chris." They showed her campaign stops interrupted by hecklers, and her opponents, particularly Bill de Blasio, gaining traction with the public. We watch the mood in Chris's campaign van darken as she rides in silence.

By the summer of that year, Chris had sunk in the polls, going from front-runner status to underdog; having been the speaker of the City Council and close ally of outgoing Mayor Bloomberg, she had begun to be perceived as an insider at a time when the city was hungry for change. Voters were frustrated with Bloomberg and wanted to elect someone significantly different, and Chris didn't differentiate herself enough from the old guard.[2] The *New York Times* documentary crew caught that frustration and much more on film, including on primary night, in her holding room at the Dream Hotel in the Chelsea section of Manhattan. The Dream Hotel was the scene of many important Chris Quinn events, from her kickoff announcement to fundraising gatherings and parties. As I entered the building on primary night, knowing what the outcome would be, it felt like the place should be re-branded the Nightmare Hotel. In the end, Chris's loss was a stunning defeat. Our early front-runner finished at the back of the Democratic pack with only 7 percent of the vote.

Days later, when I watched the documentary ultimately titled, *Hers to Lose: A Look at Christine Quinn's Failed Campaign for Mayor,* I saw the intimate account of what was happening in Chris's holding room upstairs in the hotel that night. The crew zoomed close-up shots of Chris's face as she steeled herself to address her loyal campaign workers. It's hard to watch. The off-camera reporter asks her, "What are you thinking now?" She looks into the camera, takes off her lapel microphone, and says, "I'm not answering that." A campaign staffer steps in front of the camera. Not only was Chris's loss painful, but it was televised for all to see.

The Chris Quinn documentary makes clear that recording legacy is never without risk. While the film and the primary did not represent the outcomes any of us on the campaign had hoped for, I feel it was worth the risk. Chris's run *was* historic. It was worth documenting, if only for the women and gay people who will run for mayor in the future, for any political office, and for any party or platform. It was informative, perhaps not in the ways I had hoped, but useful nonetheless. As a postmortem of a failed campaign, there is much for future candidates to learn from, including the strategies that worked to derail Chris's run. Up-and-comers can apply the film's lessons to their own efforts at winning competitive races. In the election that followed, four women were in the race for New York City mayor in 2021, which is often described as the second toughest job in America.

By knowing where pitfalls may lie and what has come before them, breakthrough communicators can better avoid them. Indeed, we often learn more from our failures than successes. I have. Even though it comes with risk, look for ways to create a permanent document of your major decisions in digestible ways that future team members and leaders can access and learn from—whether a film, written documentation, or images. While you can't force anyone to look at or learn from anything, you can rest assured you've done your best to provide relevant information to future generations.

Record History for Those to Come

I admire companies that dedicate the time and expense to record their histories. Consider American Express's legacy tied to the Pony Express tradition that allowed voyagers and their valuables to travel safely. The American Express values of reliability and accountability have long permeated the company's credit card and travel business. They were present in the days after 9/11 that I wrote about earlier. Kenneth Chenault's pitch-perfect speech to employees that both defined reality and offered hope became a rallying cry for the city and the larger business community.

Chenault had just taken the reins of American Express months earlier. About five thousand Amex employees worked in lower Manhattan, and eleven died in the attacks. In 2002, the company issued a one-year retrospective; an elegant hardback book titled *Remembrance and Renewal: American Express After 9/11* to all employees. The dedication page reads, "This is the story of a company and its extraordinary people. It begins with terror, destruction, and death. It describes acts of courage, love, and caring. It speaks to character, resolve, strength and commitment. Above all, it is a story about moving forward—last year, this year, and in the years to come. This is the story of American Express. This is your story."

The book connects the dots of the searing memory of one of the darkest days to the company's bright future. Reading it twenty years after the attack, it holds up extraordinarily well as testimony to the day, the impacted lives, and the struggle to rebuild. It's reflecting and honoring at its best. It's moving and motivational. It is also instructive for anyone who must manage and communicate during and after a crisis.

While it may feel daunting, especially in moments of hardship or crisis, to find the time and energy to memorialize your work, do it. There is help: some firms have the sole purpose of helping companies and individuals preserve their legacies. I'm familiar with several who frame and capture the traditions and backstories that illuminated their clients' histories. These firms bring their expertise in interviewing and editing to their work with an eye toward helping their clients pass on values and wisdom to perpetuate success and build their legacy.

These firms intrigue me, and I both watch and try to support their success. They facilitate memories that illuminate our future. But it doesn't require a team of experts, film crews, and ghostwriters to celebrate and mark the trail of your personal journey. You can do it yourself. My friend Jonathan Capehart did.

A Tribute to an Uncle

I met Jonathan Capehart when I was in Los Angeles during the 2000 Democratic Convention and was introduced to him by a friend of a friend. We made a date for breakfast. I remember the day clearly, how he strode across the café in his crisp white shirt, slender hand extended, and flashing one of his beautiful smiles. I suspect most people can recall the moment they met Jonathan because he is so charismatic.

That morning, in a hotel coffee shop, we talked more than ate. I was excited at the chance to know him. Like most accomplished journalists, Jonathan asked probing questions. We traded political gossip and began a friendship that now spans more than two decades. I've watched his career flourish. The year before we met, Jonathan won a Pulitzer Prize for a series of editorials that condemned the financial management of the acclaimed Harlem's Apollo Theater. He is also a member of the prestigious *Washington Post* editorial board and was promoted to associate editor in March 2022. In addition to his editorial gig, for many years Jonathan has hosted *Cape Up with Jonathan Capehart* (now rebranded as *Capehart*) a podcast that "talks with newsmakers who challenge your ideas on politics, and explore how race, religion, age, gender and cultural identity are redrawing the lines that both divide and unite America." I am a devoted listener.

So, I thought I knew Jonathan; his depths and talents were familiar to me. That perception changed on December 13, 2020, when Jonathan launched his own television show, MSNBC's *The Sunday Show*. What impressed me was not that Jonathan had been named anchor of a prime-time slot on the cable news network. He'd been an MSNBC contributor for years and was a nimble, insightful TV man. What blew me away was that Jonathan shared a deeply personal saga in the inaugural show.

Jonathan chose to remember, reflect, and honor the people that had made his breakthrough possible. His opening lines were among the most compelling television I've ever watched. It's five minutes and forty-five seconds of heart-moving, high-impact recollection.

"Many of you know me for more than a decade as a contributor at MSNBC. But most of you don't know my story, how a big-head kid from New Jersey made his way to this moment. . . . Since I was 10 years old, I wanted to be a journalist, a news commentator as I called it," Jonathan said. He goes on to explain that he became a huge news nerd, regularly watching the *Today* show as a kid. "But it wasn't until Bryant Gumbel succeeded Tom Brokaw on the show in 1982 that I saw someone who looked like me doing the job." Jonathan is African American too.

Jonathan continued to explain that no one from his family had ever worked in journalism. "The closest I got was my uncle, McKinley Branch, who was an electrician at NBC's headquarters." His uncle let him come see the studio set. "There, sitting on a sofa, I worked up the courage to talk to the woman sitting at the desk across from me." The woman turned out to be a producer, and she asked him the question all adults ask kids, "What do you want to be when you grow up?"

And Jonathan told the producer "everything . . . including how I wanted to be the next Bryant Gumbel." When it was time to go, Jonathan thanked her, and she gave him a note with the name Kay Bradley and her phone number on it. Handing him the note, the woman said, "Get yourself an internship on the *Today* show." And Jonathan did.

When he was old enough, for two summers he worked as an intern with "giants in the field." By 1992, Jonathan was back at the *Today* show as a researcher. Jonathan then took his inaugural *Sunday Show* audience through his professional ascent over a decade of jobs in journalism and television with humility.

"And now, I am the anchor of my own show," his voice cracked with emotion. He brushed away a tear. He reminded viewers that he was a "big-headed kid with a dream and no road map, only the encouragement of my mom, and a family who patiently listened while I dreamed aloud, including an uncle whose kindness put me on the right path."

I reached out to Jonathan to ask him about his decision to begin his show with a personal reflection and asked why he chose to start in this way.

He said, "For me, it wasn't even a decision to be made. Achieving my own show was such a dream since childhood, and I hadn't forgotten all those who helped me. I had to thank and name all of those people—and these folks aren't known—but for me it was important to recognize and honor the people who did things big and small to help me get to where I am."

Jonathan said the response and impact of his revelation was gratifying:

> So many people emailed, texted, reached out by Facebook messenger, connected however they could find me. The reaction was overwhelmingly positive. People were moved and touched that I shared my story and was willing to be emotional on television, which is still odd for a newsperson. But I feel everything. It's important for people to see that and to know that this person they are watching on television is a human being, a three-dimensional person with feelings, and to strip away this notion that just because I'm on television, I'm some omnipotent, omniscient, unfeeling cardboard cut-out. There's a real

person here and this person recognizes and understands that this role is one of great trust. It is a privilege and an honor to be in this position and I needed people to understand that I recognize that every single Sunday, every time I'm on the air. It keeps my feet on the ground and puts it all in perspective.

By sharing his memories, Jonathan revealed his truest self. His vulnerability led to credibility. He also very well may have inspired young people with aspirations for careers like Jonathan's that anything is possible, no matter your background. This groundbreaking, award-winning communicator personalized his work and built trust by reflecting and honoring.

Reflecting Is a Team Sport

Not many of us get a chance to reflect on national television as Jonathan did or have a documentary company follow us around. Most of us share our stories in smaller, more private settings. Shortly after the Covid-19 vaccine was launched, I began a series of reflective conversations on the breakthrough theme with my team. The only agenda was to create a forum for honoring past achievements and imagining what new heights we could reach.

Each session was intimate, a small group of five or six colleagues from across the division. I sent no pre-reads and showed no Power-Point presentations. We were faces from across the globe, in squares on the computer screen. I saw in everyone's eyes what I felt in my heart—a desire to stay close to one another and to the powerful feeling of accomplishment that we enjoyed during the race to develop, manufacture, and distribute the vaccine. We didn't want to let those feelings go, but to reflect and restore ourselves to be poised for more bold moves.

"Let's each share a breakthrough, either professional or personal, that was meaningful to us," I said at the start of each session. I heard several stories of professional achievement ranging from those who were onboarded to the company during the remote working period to those who found meaningful ways to achieve self-care while locked down. I marveled at the agility of those who started a new job and learned to swim in the corporate slipstream while we worked remotely. That couldn't have been easy. Others talked about the intensity of being on the frontlines of the vaccine rollout in countries worldwide. These colleagues were responding to anxious government officials, answering aggressive questions from the media, and liaising with advocacy groups for patients in other disease areas who feared being ignored while the world was riveted to Covid. Cancer, heart disease, and all the other horrid afflictions didn't go on hiatus during Covid. "Pressure is a privilege—it only comes to those who earn it," I reminded the team, quoting one of my heroes, tennis legend and social activist Billie Jean King.

More often, my colleagues reflected on personal changes sparked by the pandemic and its impact on their lives, most especially working remotely. One man in his midthirties finally learned to drive a car and got his license. A woman who no longer had to spend hours commuting to the office took up playing the piano. Another woman confessed her surprise over the joy she found in seeing her three small children more during the day. Self-described as an assertive career woman, the time spent at home and in her household flow gave her a greater feeling of balance between her professional and personal selves. There were lots of stories of loving rescue dogs and first-time gardeners.

"I'm no longer blond," I said. At the onset of the pandemic, I began to watch little estuaries of silver trickle through my hair. I cheered their progress. I considered making the break from years of coloring my hair a perfected honey-wheat blond with ribbons of natural-looking highlights. Against the backdrop of life-and-death decisions made during the coronavirus pandemic, my decision may have seemed trivial. But for me, it was a meaningful, pivotal call. Like many women, I began to color my hair as I made my career in corporate America. As some of my features began to shift and sag with age, my beautifully coiffed blond bob became my prized signature look. I don't know who wrote the rules of women's hair, but I've obeyed them. For women in big corporations, the code is clear—no gray hair please.

Today I love my full head of gray hair. It's a symbol—a demarcation of my life before and after the Covid crisis. My new appearance was forged in the sorrow and pain of the pandemic. A daily reminder of my ninety-three-year-old mother-in-law's struggle to survive in a senior center rampant with the disease, of my young adult daughter's forced return home from her graduate school when her university shuttered, and of my cousin's anguish at having to close the restaurant he spent his life building. The silver streaks on my head keep these losses top of mind, literally.

My new wild hair makes the pandemic's mark permanent. It signifies that I have emerged from a devasting time transformed. My silver mane stands for courage and strength. I published an essay in *Time* magazine on the transformation of my hair and heart, posing the idea that the gray wisps that had sprung forth along my hairline and feathered from my temples might be wings. I believe they were.

I shared all of this with my team in these reflection sessions. Why? Because in the work-from-home era, the personal and professional worlds melded together. Authenticity is essential as a communicator and leader. These truths—of struggle and triumph—draw us closer. The deep reflection that honors your wins and owns your failures will lead to the most meaningful storytelling.

The Last Word

It may be strange to talk about funerals and eulogies in a book about business communications, but death is often when the ultimate story of a person is told. Publications like the *New York Times* and the *Economist* are known for their brilliant obits and instructive cultural and personal histories that provide readers with insight, inspiration, and lessons in living. The renowned former obituary writer for the *Times*, Margalit Fox, said, "People have a primal fear of death, but 98 percent of the obit has nothing to do with death, but with life. There are maybe two sentences in there about when or where the guy died and with the rest, you let the person's life guide the treatment. We like to say it's the jolliest department in the paper."[3]

The best obituaries are of course not a complete record of a person's life, but it is often as close an outsider can come to both a summary of its highlights and a review of triumphs and tragedies. They offer lessons, ways of expressing important achievements, and chronicling failures with empathy and hindsight. These are important skills for the breakthrough communicator.

When the legendary Estée Lauder died in 2004 at the age of ninety-eight, I had worked for the cosmetic company for about eight years. By the time I came on board, Estée Lauder had stepped back from public life, and regrettably, I never had a chance to meet her in person. However, her persona was imbued in the offices where I worked, and you could feel her influence throughout the company, where her office was kept intact as if she had just left it to attend a luncheon appointment. The stories about her grit and grace were legendary. When she passed away, I had the privilege of helping facilitate her funeral, held at Lincoln Center in Manhattan. The event included 2,400 guests, and the New York Pops played a medley of her favorite songs as black-and-white images of her life flashed on a large screen set up in the hall.[4]

A roster of remarkable people whom she counted among her friends, including Barbara Walters, Michael Bloomberg, and others, gave a series of eulogies. Afterward, treats included two of her favorite foods: marshmallows and champagne. Honoring her legacy was both a family and a company event. It was a powerful example of communicating the importance of someone's life and celebrating them in a variety of ways: through words, images, music, and food. It was in perfect keeping with the culture of the company she founded.

The obituary is an appraisal of life and a record of its highs and lows as a way of illuminating why that life was significant. Writing one makes you think twice about less obvious moments in a person's life, which may be where the most useful insights and ideas are found. It helps you assess cultural values of the past and how they intersect with modern mores. This is useful practice for all kinds of breakthrough communication, which seeks to delight, surprise, and educate.

What would you put in your own obit? It may seem like a morbid task, but give it a go. To up the challenge, keep it between 750 and 1,500 words. Resist the urge to use Victorian clichés ("He touched everyone who met him," "She was surrounded by the love of family and friends") and instead focus on the pivotal points in your life and what made them so—your first job and how it informed your future career; mistakes that became pathways to new adventures; trips that changed your perspective; relationships that altered your course. This is an obituary that sums up your life and its meaning and frames you within the time you lived. If you are brave enough, have access to them, and they are willing, interview people from your past and current life—old friends, teachers, employers, colleagues.

This exercise forces you to focus on the details that are important within the context you are writing and to choose between what is essential and what can be left out. Editing in this way makes you a better communicator—more succinct, focused, and sympathetic to the reader.

Why History Matters for Breakthrough Communication

Founding values form the heart of an organization, no matter how old or young your business. Understanding the best and worst of your legacy makes your communications more trustworthy, more meaningful, and better understood and accepted. Reflecting on values and successes can guide communications efforts.

Why you need to fully understand your legacy:

- *You can call on your organization's growth, milestones, and significant triumphs.* Successes are built on the efforts of mission-driven leadership, hardworking staff, supportive communities, and customers and stakeholders. When Pfizer hit the first billion doses of the vaccine produced and distributed, it was a celebratory moment. It motivated staff and other stakeholders to take stock of the meaning of their work. In the future, this and other similar moments are useful in inspiring and motivating. In effect, it is an active way of saying, if we could rise to the tough challenge then, we can do it again.

- *You can speak to how you overcame defeat and hardship.* No company or person accomplished anything without failures. Resiliency is an important part of storytelling; everyone loves the hero's tales of overcoming setbacks. It gives stories richness and texture—along with authenticity and trust. Albert Bourla has willingly and courageously shared his parents' story of narrowly escaping the Holocaust, and this humanizes him to people who may see him as an arm's length CEO, which he isn't at all. It is also important to understand and recognize failures when communicating effectively—with humbleness and empathy. Failure or errors are nothing to be ashamed of *if* you have learned from them and communicate those lessons clearly and with humility.

- *You can chronicle the impact on the communities served.* Every company has an economic and social impact on the community where it was founded and the communities where it operates. That means that both the successes and the shortcomings of a company are felt—either directly or indirectly—by the people of those communities. Mindful business histories respect community relationships and record them in terms of how both the company and the community changed over the years. For instance, Silicon Valley and Big Tech have a unique relationship, and the community we recognize today in Northern California could only be possible in that specific location. Hewlett-Packard started in 1939 in a garage in Palo Alto. The Santa Clara Valley (as Silicon Valley was once known) was a largely agricultural area and unpopulated, but close to a large city (San Francisco). There were also many trade schools nearby and two world-class universities: Stanford and Berkeley.[5] The corporate history of every Silicon Valley company is tied in one way or another to the location and post-WWII events that encouraged migration to the West and as such should not be ignored. Likewise, for companies that sprang up in other places, from Maine to Manhattan, Palo Alto to Peoria.

From a communicator's perspective, people helped is a better metric than money made. You do not count success in dollars and cents, but how your product or service improves the lives of the people it serves and makes their lives safer, better, and more enjoyable. This has been a shift at Pfizer—we now communicate first in human terms: how many lives impacted, as in hospital stays averted or babies protected through vaccination. Then we turn to sales and profit numbers.

- *You can make your company's messaging more authentic.*
  There is a significant gap between the messaging of most brands and their prospective customers—and the data doesn't lie: 53 percent of consumers don't trust brands until they experience or can see real-life proof of their claims. Heritage builds trust in communications. By infusing legacy messaging in your communications with consumers, clients, and customers, you instill a sense of trust. That's one of the reasons why companies put founding dates (i.e., "since 1877") on their signs, doors, stationery, and advertising.

- *You can develop and strengthen company culture.* Company culture matters. It's the force that attracts new talent, builds morale, inspires innovation, and ultimately communicates to customers that you are worthy of their trust. The history of a business can be compelling to prospective talent and customers. Culture has to be lived, not just written, over time.

So, stop and take a moment, or as much time as needed, to place yourself and your ideas in the constellation of your work universe. Try to honor all the precedents, bold thinking, and creative inputs that came before you. That reflection will set your communications on a powerful path guided by wisdom and perspective.

CHAPTER TEN

Why Is Everybody So Angry?

Seek Harmony

"THE SECRET SERVICE HAS CLEARED ME TO TELL YOU THIS, but you must promise not to tell anyone else," Albert said on a phone call with me in February of 2021. "President Biden is coming to visit our Kalamazoo factory next week. We better start planning."

What?! President Biden was making his first domestic trip since his swearing-in, and he was coming to see us? I could hardly believe it. What greater evidence could there be to prove that we had broken through? For years, no public official wanted to be anywhere near a Big Pharma company and would certainly never agree to a joint media event.

Now, thanks to our vaccine and our constructive engagements with the White House, that antagonism had been set aside. It was exhilarating to put the battle between Big Pharma and politicians—and especially the public—in the rearview mirror, even if it could be temporary.

The president would be traveling on *Air Force One* to our plant to meet our workers. Albert and I would be there to greet him. My first instinct was to pick up the phone and tell every one of my friends. Thankfully, I paused. Remembering the heavy price I had paid for divulging a confidence so long ago and understanding the importance of preserving the president's security, I wisely kept my big trap shut. I discussed it with no one outside the circle of colleagues who had also been cleared by the Secret Service and told of the visit.

There were a lot of moving parts involved to make the trip a success. If the communication plan wasn't executed properly, chaos and disappointment could result. Those outcomes were not options, as far as I was concerned. My breakthrough strategies were going to help ensure a positive news day for all. My efforts in the days that followed drew heavily on all the principles I've expressed here.

What would be my goal for this historic visit? I didn't feel we needed to be overly scripted or performative in our comments. The president had his ambitions and we had ours—aligned but not necessarily the same. The White House team seemed focused on showing the new president engaged and in charge of the ongoing Covid crisis. We wanted to showcase our factory and our dedicated employees. These aren't identical goals, but they are complementary, and we could both come out on top. We could have parallel interests. That would be good enough. I felt satisfied that we could strive for harmony.

"Harmony is the pleasing arrangement of different tones, voices or instruments, not the combination of identical sounds," wrote Adam Grant, one of the world's most influential management thinkers, on his LinkedIn page. With a goal of harmony in mind, I was confident that despite some differences of opinion between us and the president and his administration, we could achieve a shared and coherent view of the Covid challenge and even align on some next steps. I wasn't asking for total agreement. We didn't have to parrot one another's words or have those "identical sounds" Grant references. All we needed to do was to share the experience in a respectful, synchronized way. I believe this is the stance that mature, conscientious communicators take toward high-stakes encounters. Unanimity would be nice, but harmony is enough.

First, I would not fail to prepare.

Every step President Biden took in the four square miles that comprised the building had to be negotiated and choreographed with his advance team before they would approve it. We laid short strips of blue tape at various locations across the floor signaling where the president would stand and where we would stand, too. Social distancing and camera angles both had to be considered. We made contingency plans should anything—from Michigan's icy weather to its extreme politics—interfere with our carefully laid plans.

Through planning and attention to detail, I hoped to build trust with the president's highly protective staffers. My communications had to be honest and clear. They asked what seemed like zillions of detailed questions, all of which I answered quickly and candidly.

"Is your Kalamazoo plant a union site?"

"No."

"Can you assure us that the president's visit will not delay any vaccine production?"

"Yes."

And so, it went for days. As soon as one question was addressed, another was volleyed our way.

"We want to see where the vaccine vials are filled," the Biden advanced team woman requested. That is a dramatic, visual part of the factory line. It's the money shot that is often seen on TV.

"Sure, happy to," I said. "We will need to build in time to gown up and wear a hairnet," I said on a conference call with several Biden team members on the line.

Silence.

"Hello," I asked, wondering if I'd lost the phone connection.

"The president will not wear a hairnet," came the reply.

I'm familiar enough with the manufacturing rules to know this was nonnegotiable. We were at a standoff. I feared the Biden staffers would pull the plug on the trip. Our glorious moment would be over before it began.

I needed some original thinking. Surely the team that had found a manufacturing solution to a novel vaccine could help here. They leaped in. We let go of the vial-filling visual by creating a better one. We moved the glistening new machines that had been invented, patented, and built in less than a year and lined them up in a way to make a powerful statement of American manufacturing ingenuity. The Kalamazoo manufacturing crew figured it out. The Biden people signed off on the hastily arranged new plan to spotlight that cool technology, and the presidential visit stayed on the calendar. I was relieved (I don't look so hot in a hairnet either).

The night before the trip, I couldn't sleep. I turned every detail over in my mind.

I was out of bed before my 5 a.m. wake-up alarm. Soon after, I was in the car and on my way to arrive early at the airport. Schlepping my computer backpack, an overnight bag in case we got stuck on the ground, and a large thermos of coffee—the necessities of life on the road—I met up with my small traveling party: Albert, of course—a meeting like this could not fail to include our CEO; Yolanda Lyle, his chief of staff; and Mike McDermott, Pfizer's head of global manufacturing.

Our destination, Kalamazoo, is a small town tucked into the northwestern corner of Michigan. It's home to the manufacturing facility that makes our Covid vaccine and, on most days, a quiet place. On that morning, it would play host to recently inaugurated President Joe Biden, his senior staff, and the presidential press corps.

When I was boarding, I realized this was the first time I'd stepped on a plane in nearly a year. Travel, a pleasure I had previously taken for granted, was now something to savor. I was happy to be in transit, to be moving again. The motion itself was uplifting.

As I felt the plane begin to descend, I looked out the window at the hard, frozen ground. Farms appeared below like uneven patches on a quilt. The landing gear rumbled as it lowered from the plane's belly. We touched down.

Driving to the factory over the barren interstates that led to smaller roads dotted with McDonald's, Hampton Inns, and local pizza places, I was reminded of home. Not New York City, my current place of residence, but where I was born, Missouri. I knew it had been too long since I'd been back to see the few elderly relatives that still live there. The pandemic taught me many lessons, including the importance of family. I made a mental note to plan a trip soon.

We'd started traveling so early that day, it was still morning when we arrived in Kalamazoo. The town was waking up, people were shoveling the previous night's snowfall off their sidewalks, coaxing their car engines to turn over in the bitter cold. These were the people I imagined our vaccines protecting. I jotted a few feelings of joy in my journal. Gratitude for having been involved in the vaccine was coursing through my veins.

We arrived at the seventy-year-old manufacturing plant. Steam was billowing from its smokestacks. Three flags flew crisply near the front door. At the top was an oversized American flag; in the middle was a sharp white Pfizer flag bearing the new corporate logo that we had launched less than two months earlier. Also waving proudly in the wind was a Black Lives Matter flag. As a statement against the racial violence the previous summer, we decided to fly the BLM flags on all our company sites in the United States during February, Black History Month. The three flags were a collage of symbols reflecting patriotism, originality, courage, and pride.

Once inside the building, we shook the snow off our boots, hung up our heavy jackets, and gathered with the local team to review plans one more time.

Soon thereafter, right on schedule, President Biden and his entourage came in via the loading dock due to security measures. Albert greeted the president and then presented the team. "Let me introduce Sally Susman," Albert said to the president. "In my administration, she is the secretary of state." I was delighted that Albert described my role as his diplomat and emissary.

I had prepared to make the most of my few moments. After all, how many chances do we get in life to meet the leader of the free world? Not many. I am not so sophisticated that I won't admit to being giddy. Of course, I told the president how honored we were to receive him on his first domestic trip. But I wanted to connect with empathy. So, I pivoted to a personal point. "I was deeply moved by your book, *Promise Me, Dad*," I said, referencing his recent memoir about the death of his beloved son Beau. I explained that my motivation to join a health-care company was to be a part of cures for the horrible cancer that had taken his son. "We as a company are driven to spare other families from similar tragedies," I said. The president and I were both double-masked and standing six feet apart, but our eyes met. We communed for a moment, connected.

Then the president and a gaggle of his team and ours snaked through the plant. Curiosity held me back. I wanted to spend our limited time together with two young women who were essential to the inner workings of the White House: White House spokeswoman Jen Psaki and the president's campaign manager and political adviser, Jen O'Malley. I admire them. Jen O'Malley was the first female to lead a presidential campaign and navigated it beautifully to victory. Jen Psaki had, from her first White House press conference, demonstrated so many breakthrough communications principles: preparedness, humility, and perfect pitch. Following on the heels of President Trump's distant relationship and rare engagements with the press, Psaki set a new tone. At the end of her first briefing on January 20, Jen stood at the White House press podium and said, "Let's do it again tomorrow."

Trailing behind President Biden and Albert, we walked through the midcentury plant, revealing at each turn, a high-tech world of new machines designed and built in the past twelve months in our race to produce the vaccine. We wandered past manufacturing lines, quality checks, packaging tools, and then through the freezer farm, a vast warehouse of massive containers storing the vaccine at –70 C.

"Hi, I'm Joe," the president said, as he greeted each worker along the line. As a humane and high-touch communicator and connector, he showed great humility.

"Tell me, what do you do?" President Biden asked several folks on the plant floor. It wasn't a talking point. He was truly curious. To me, he looked so slight, almost fragile, with his suit hanging from his narrow frame. Still, he focused on whoever he was with, taking the time to listen and learn.

Following the tour, we held a press conference in front of those gleaming machines. Albert's introduction and remarks were carefully prepared. He announced to the president, and the world, via the reporters in the large press pool, some very good news. We were rapidly stepping up production, and delivery levels would double in the coming weeks. Also, we'd solved the temperature challenge, and the vaccine no longer had stability issues, allowing it to be stored for longer times outside ultra-cold conditions. That meant that we could soon begin shipping to smaller pharmacies and reach more remote areas. The press took notes.

Then the president spoke and reiterated his commitment to vaccinate 100 million people in his first one hundred days in office. This simple, powerful vision was a phrase from his inaugural address, the language of a master communicator. Moreover, he continued to repeat, for emphasis, his inspiring vision.

The president went on to talk about the "miracle of manufacturing" and described our work as "the most difficult operational challenge the nation has ever faced."

"At every stage, safety is the utmost priority." He continued, "The whole process takes teamwork, precision, and around the clock focus." And he admired "pioneering technologies that less than a year ago were little more than theories and aspirations."

I was still astonished that a newly minted president would choose our site to make his first trip. Before this—before the pandemic, the vaccine race, and our breakthrough communications—this scene would have been unimaginable. The press coverage that followed was extraordinary. Several networks covered the visits and speeches in their entirety. We were not only making history but shaping opinions as to the value big biopharma companies can bring to society.

The president said one more thing, addressing the public in front of the TV camera, that stuck with me: "We are still in the teeth of the pandemic." I knew he was right, and I was grateful to him for having the courage to speak the truth. The pandemic's bite was rendered less painful because of the president's candid and empathetic words.

When our flight touched down that evening in New York, I knew I had enjoyed a halcyon day. Surely, in the future, we will not always agree with the president or see the world at such an eye-to-eye level. Inevitably there will be disagreements over policies, regulations, pricing, and more. But I am confident we will create harmony in the future—not every note has to be in sync to sound good.

About two weeks after the Kalamazoo trip, a large manila envelope with the return address "The White House" appeared in my mailbox. Enclosed was a photo of the president, Albert, and me in the plant along with a lovely letter that said, among other thoughts, "I want to express my gratitude for all of your hard work in making my visit a success and accompanying me on the tour." He continued, "We are forever grateful and will keep you in our prayers." The president is a generous thank-you-note writer.

The coming together of people and the understanding we achieved that day were a direct result of the breakthrough communications principles I describe in this book. Achieving harmony requires intention, courage, preparation, and reflection. I felt we had exemplified those principles.

With a sigh of relief and a deep breath of pride at what we had accomplished, it hit me that it was almost exactly one year from the night that I'd wandered through Manhattan terrified by the uncertainty of some new virus, hunting for toilet paper and fearing for my family.

Now that fear was subsiding. Anxiety was being replaced by relief as vaccines were being administered across the country. My company had been the one to lead the effort. I'd been on the team from start to finish.

Discordance

The peacefulness was short-lived. In the months that followed, there was plenty of blowback, especially in the United States where everything in the Covid response from mask policies to vaccine distribution had been politicized. The country was deeply divided. When I was out in my community wearing my Pfizer sweatshirt and someone would stop me and ask if I work at the company, I would always say yes and then wait to see which way it unfolded. It could be a hug and stories about how the vaccine let them see their grandma after a year, allowed their kid to go to school, or just let them sleep at night. Or it could be an angry diatribe with allegations that we were in a "plandemic" wrought by the pharma companies to insert microchips in people and profit from fear. Sigh.

While Pfizer proved our mantra that "Science Will Win" with uncontestable clinical results and real-world data, it appeared that perhaps the communications campaign had been lost. We had not created confidence or convinced large swaths of the public. Indeed, significant segments of the population remained staunchly vaccine-resistant.[1] Meanwhile, some of the most powerful voices and influential names, many in our own government and even health organizations, offered conflicting advice about masking policies, which therapies to trust, and social distancing requirements.[2] I like to think this was often not the result of malice but the pressure that results when people desperately want information about a situation that was not clearly understood, even by the experts who were studying it.

Arguments and data points about our efforts to provide the vaccine at a price that ensured access for all sometimes fell on deaf ears. In the winter of 2021, as the virus persisted and new variants surfaced, anxiety and anger were once again on the rise. Dr. Tedros Adhanom Ghebreyesus, leader of the World Health Organization, an important stakeholder in global health, and someone we worked with closely, voiced concern that the rapid booster rollouts in the West were a return to "vaccine hoarding" and would exacerbate vaccine inequity.[3] Seth Berkley, CEO of the vaccine alliance Gavi, a UN-backed effort to get vaccines to developing countries, said in December 2021 that he was seeing signs that rich countries were withholding vaccine donations out of fear of the omicron variant and described the behavior as "Inequity 2.0."[4]

There were scary moments of public unrest. Fights broke out on airlines, and angry passengers argued with one another and flight attendants over mask-wearing rules. Restaurant patrons grew unruly standing in long lines in the cold, waiting to present proof of vaccination.

It became clear that vaccine mandates would be required to reach the critical level of "herd immunity." Many significant employers, ranging from the airlines to municipalities across the country, began to require their workers show proof of vaccination to keep their jobs. Pfizer had encouraged colleagues to vaccinate since it earned approval, and by the summer of 2021, 90 percent of our employees had voluntarily taken the shots. Ultimately, we too implemented a mandate, as many across business and society were watching our moves. If the company that made the vaccine wasn't requiring its employees to vaccinate, it would undermine our efforts and those of others. I had hoped we wouldn't have to come to that conclusion, but I understood and supported why we did.

Forcing people to do anything is rarely a winning strategy. Opening minds and moving hearts shouldn't involve twisting arms or breaking spirits. The vaccine mandates only made angry people angrier. It made skeptics more skeptical: if it's such a great idea, why do you have to force people to do it? Detractors dug in and doubled down in opposition.

In September of 2021, President Biden issued new rules that required businesses with more than a hundred workers to ensure their employees were vaccinated by January 4, 2022. The mandate would have covered 84 million employees. The response? Protests were held across the country and eleven attorneys general filed lawsuits. Within two weeks of the mandate deadline, the US Supreme Court blocked the Biden administration's vaccine mandate for large employers.

"I am disappointed that the Supreme Court has chosen to block common-sense life-saving requirements for employees at large businesses that were grounded squarely in both science and the law," President Biden responded in a January 13, 2022, statement from the White House. We shall see how the outcome of further legal wrangling and regulations writing unfolds, but in my experience, coercion is not the road to consensus.

Cacophony

Following the vaccine mandates, some Pfizer colleagues felt the heat personally, the animosity bombarding their daily lives. Josh Brown, Pfizer's vice president for state government affairs, came under personal attack.

Josh is plain-spoken and earnest, so an unlikely target. For years, I watched Josh be greeted warmly by governors on both sides of the political aisle. He's not a partisan, just a man focused on advocating for science and patients. Josh is humble and hardworking. He has a firm handshake and an open manner.

In August of 2021, the gentleman who represented Josh's school district announced he was going to resign. That created a vacancy to be filled by an appointment of the county commission. Josh was encouraged to seek the appointment, and in late September his county commissioners nominated him for the role. The next step would be the vote by the full commission to give him the appointment. Everything seemed on track and straightforward.

The news of Josh's nomination set off outrage and negative social media posts. The concern was that, because he worked for Pfizer, his agenda would be to promote mandatory vaccinations for all children in the school system. This is notwithstanding the fact that Josh had stated that he would recuse himself from any votes (including those related to vaccines) that conflicted with his work at Pfizer.

On October 11, the county commission met to vote on Josh's nomination. During the public comment period, ten people spoke against him. The arguments included cronyism—he was only being considered because people on the commission had known him a long time; that as a lobbyist for Pfizer, his job is to push vaccines and that's what he would do on the school board; that his appointment was political payback because he helped many of the current members get elected (this was true of only a few of them). Some speakers used a tone that was nasty and mean-spirited. All this happened in front of his wife, children, and parents, who were in the audience. It was an all-too-real example of how bitter and divisive politics and the issues surrounding vaccines had become. Ultimately, the commission voted sixteen to three to approve Josh's nomination, and he's serving with distinction on the school board.

For Josh, things have calmed down significantly. The state legislature acted to take some of these vaccine-related decisions out of the hands of the local school boards, which helped lower the temperature.

But I credit Josh for managing his way through this quagmire by relying on several of the principles in this book.

Josh was *intentional* about his reasons for stepping into the public square. He enjoys politics and policy-making, but the rationale for why he raised his hand for public office at that delicate moment when health-care policy and return-to-school protocols were on the line was also personal. "I've got three kids in public school," he said.

Josh *paused and prepared* before entering the arena by talking to the commissioners who would decide his fate. As a longtime resident of the area, he asked them frankly, "How would you view my candidacy?" He didn't want to put them in an awkward position or make their job harder or compromise their political position.

He thought about the *pitch* he would need during this heated election. Josh told me that "anyone who knows me knows I don't have many high highs or low lows. I'm pretty even keeled. One of the things this situation didn't need was someone who would come in and be really emotional, because all this right now is pure emotion." He explained, "What we needed was someone who would come in and listen and be measured, so tone mattered a lot to me. I needed to say the right things and say them in the right way."

Josh is not an average politician. It was the reason he almost didn't do it. He generally stays out of the spotlight, not in it. When it became obvious that his nomination was generating a lot of attention, and he became the subject of news stories and social media posts, that started to bother him, and he questioned whether he really wanted this attention. "That's not my style. Humility is the way I'm wired," Josh said. In the end, Josh's *humility*, like that of all breakthrough communicators, proved an essential asset.

Josh found a lighthearted moment to help manage the stress. "We hadn't told the kids what we were going to do that night at the commission meeting. They knew I was looking to be on the school board, but they didn't realize we were headed into a meeting about it." Josh told me that he wanted them to be aware that it would be a large meeting of people holding signs, and some of them would be loud. Why? Because they didn't want their dad to be on the school board. Why? "We went through the elementary version of the issue and that it's OK to have different opinions," he said. It was a civics lesson offered during a twenty-minute ride in his Honda Odyssey minivan.

"You are going to see tonight why it's great to live in America," he told them. "People are going to go to the podium and say things they really believe and say things about me you probably won't like. Hopefully they will be polite and use nice words, but they might not. This is what's great about living in America—we all get to say what we want." It made it easier for them when they got to a room of three hundred people, many of whom said negative things about Josh. His children listened and smiled. The commissioners voted. Some other candidates received a few votes, but more supported Josh. He was elected, and the kids got a taste of democracy in action.

Brave, Beautiful Voices

Beyond my Pfizer colleagues, other brave advocates for the vaccine were targeted. My friend Dr. Leana Wen is a public health advocate, an op-ed columnist with the *Washington Post*, and a CNN medical analyst. Her recent book, *Lifelines: A Doctor's Journey in the Fight for Public Health*, is a moving story of hardship and accomplishment. Leana is one of the most gracious, inclusive people I know. Still, she told me she receives hate mail for "being a pragmatic person and refusing to be anti–Big Pharma." In the fall of 2021, a Texas man was charged in federal court for threatening Leana for her Covid-19 vaccination advocacy, ethnic heritage, and gender. His purpose was apparently to threaten and intimidate. Thankfully, this bully did not prevail. He pleaded guilty and is awaiting sentencing. Leana continues to speak out regularly with candor and clarity on the vaccine and other important health-care topics.

Unfortunately, these sad stories are not rare. I wonder and worry why we can't disagree agreeably? Can we not debate in the public square without throwing insults? Are we not worse off after the pandemic—not only for the loss of life and economic security—but for the ways in which we tore one another down? There is significant evidence that isolation and depression persist even as Covid is in retreat and unemployment is low.

Some truly courageous leaders who communicated through the hateful clutter during this time have been exceptions to the antagonism and negativity. These are people I admire most. In addition to Dr. Wen, consider the bravery of:

Pope Francis, who avoided the usual papal preference to avoid the crosshairs of highly public and politicized issues. On August 18, 2021, His Holiness the Pope, six cardinals, and archbishops from North, Central, and South America issued a public service announcement orchestrated by the Ad Council in English, Spanish, and Portuguese to encourage Catholics to receive the vaccine. "Thanks to God's grace and to the work of many, we now have vaccines to protect us from Covid-19," Pope Francis said in the PSA. "Getting the vaccines that are authorized is an act of love. I pray to God that each one of us can make his or her own small gesture of love, no matter how small, love is always grand." These moving words were especially meaningful, as some opposed to the vaccine tried to discourage pro-life folks from taking the shot by alleging (falsely) that the mRNA vaccines included cells from aborted human embryos.

Dr. Ashish Jha, who became a near-daily voice of reason across many media outlets during the Covid crisis. The Indian American physician and dean of Brown University School of Public Health emerged as a go-to expert during the pandemic. Early on we heard that Dr. Jha had said some less-than-flattering things about the Pfizer approach to vaccine development at a meeting of the Democratic House Caucus. Rather than fume in silence and decry the vast conspiracy against us, we picked up the phone and arranged a conversation between Jha and

Albert Bourla. The two men had a candid and constructive exchange of views and I admired Jha's interest and willingness to learn more. From that moment forward, I fully admired Jha's tireless effort to educate the public. In the spring of 2022, Jha was rewarded for his efforts to lead the Covid conversation with an appointment by President Biden to be the White House coronavirus response coordinator.

Kareem Abdul-Jabbar, the seventy-five-year-old former professional basketball player who blazed a trail in the game for over twenty NBA seasons received his vaccine on television and early on was vocal about his support for the vaccine. Given the resistance of many of the leagues' most popular players, this was a bold move. "The NBA should insist all players and staff be vaccinated or remove them from the team," he said on CNN on September 28, 2021. "I don't think they are behaving like good teammates or good citizens. This is a war we are involved in. Masks and vaccines—they are the weapons that we use to fight."

Dorothy Oliver is neither a celebrity nor a medical professional. She's a strong-willed, tenacious woman who made a difference in her Panola, Alabama, community. "We went door-to-door to talk to people," she said. "You go to them calm. If you are calm, they will listen."[5] And listen they did. Oliver was responsible for getting 97 percent of the Panola residents vaccinated. For her effort, she was recognized by *USA Today* in its Best of Humankind Awards, hosted by the *Today* show's Jenna Bush Hager, and received a special message from the chief medical adviser to President Biden, Dr. Anthony Fauci, praising her "extraordinary accomplishment."

Each of these breakthrough communicators—a religious leader, a dean of public health, a former basketball legend, and a passionate neighbor—all rose to advocate for a cause. They strove for harmony, each in their own way, in persuading others, and became part of the effort to turn our world back to safety. They were the torchbearers.

I admire their courage. My nagging insecurity is not helpful as a communicator and advocate when it's important to stand strong and depersonalize. Insecurity is a liability when you find yourself in the public square. I respect those who can brush off unfounded criticisms. I knew I needed to be tougher. This would be a long game.

Looking at history, I reread President Theodore Roosevelt's speech entitled "Citizenship in a Republic," which he gave at the Sorbonne in Paris in 1910. The speech is often referred to as "The Man in the Arena" and many draw strength from the section that reads: "It's not the critic who counts; not the man who points out how the strong man stumbles or where the doer of deeds could have done better. The credit belongs to the man who is actually in the arena, whose face is marred by dust and sweat and blood . . . who spends himself in a worthy cause."

With that, I metaphorically dusted myself off, stopped worrying about the naysayers' complaints, and reminded myself what an honor it was to be in this arena. Around the same time, a friend who was a first responder at the World Trade Center after the 9/11 attack reminded me that the only thing harder than being in the middle of the crisis is being on the outskirts, unable to help.

I dug into my personal reserves and found calm, confidence, and strength that was essential to keep going. I'm proud that my company rose from the depths of a poor reputation to a top-ranked brand. In 2021, Albert Bourla was named CNN Business's CEO of the Year and *Fortune* magazine named Pfizer number four on its Most Admired Company list. Wow, from the bottom of the line-up to being among the most revered names in business.

Still, we too have miles to go, and I feel more inspired than ever to remain at the helm of our work to build trust. The greatest risks we face in that endeavor are arrogance and complacency. It's my job to safeguard us against both.

* * *

It will take a long time for the world to heal from Covid. New variants continue to emerge. Borders open and close as the pandemic continues to ebb and flow. Protective policies are waived and then reinstated. People remain on edge. There is still much work left for many to do.

The harmony I strive for does seem to be an elusive goal during times of struggle and change. In an early passage of *Don Quixote*, Orly is passing through a village in Spain with his assistant Sancho Panza when they hear a ruckus made by animals howling. "Sancho, the dogs are barking, it means we are moving forward." The same is true today, that the yelping and commotion we encounter is the sound of movement and progress. If a full armistice cannot be achieved, let's aim for harmony and the ability to live together in mutual respect.

I continue to wonder, as I look back, if I was up to the challenge. When tensions flared, I felt distressed. In truth, on occasion, I faltered. My knees went weak with the thought that the pandemic might go on for years in an endless roller coaster of new threats, allegations, and misperceptions. We'd have to keep defending and fighting back. I've never been comfortable with conflict. I'm a pleaser by nature and am easily unnerved when I think people are mad at me (which I assume they frequently are). When things go off the rails, my first thought is usually, "What did I do wrong?" Then, "What could I have done better?" So, I have unfinished business, and our story is only partly told. Still, I believe breakthroughs have occurred—those in science and those in society—by a dialogue that has opened minds along the way. Hearts have been stirred and moved; some previously considered villains have emerged as heroes. We've shape-shifted the views of many, and our impact will be lasting.

The fights over masks and vaccine mandates revealed a deep divide that is neither ephemeral nor tied to the crisis of the day. This rift isn't only about a virus and our response to it. The more troubling aspects of social and cultural change that the virus threw into high relief will take more than a particular policy vote or potent new antigen to heal. Repairing the breach will rely on the breakthrough principles. The tenets of breakthrough communications served me well during the best of times and the worst ones and will continue to steer me. They are the guideposts we should all use as we face the difficult moments that inevitably come, to keep the conversation both civil and productive.

We must be intentional and prioritize the work of bridge building. It will take courage and candor at a time when your instinct may be to run and hide. Curiosity about one another as humans with different perspectives and creativity in how we connect will be essential. Feelings of gratitude will have to supersede those of anger and suspicion. We should pause and prepare for how we want to lead in this more complicated world. Humility will be a surprising and effective response to the aggression. Humor can lift the mood and lighten the tension to allow for meaningful change. Reflecting on earlier times in our history, such as the Civil War and the fight for civil rights, when we literally bore arms against one another, may offer a pathway to peace. Seeking harmony amid discord is always a worthy pursuit.

NOTES

Chapter 2

1. Andrew Gelwicks, *The Queer Advantage: Conversations with LGBTQ+ Leaders on the Power of Identity* (Boston: Hachette Go, 2020).

2. Nell Casey, "A Look Back at 30 Years of Union Square Cafe, Which Closes This Saturday," *Gothamist*, December 11, 2015, https://gothamist.com/food/a-look-back-at-30-years-of-union-square-cafe-which-closes-this-saturday.

3. Amanda Luz Henning Santiago, "New York's Efforts to Snuff Out Smoking," *City & State*, September 16, 2019, https://www.cityandstateny.com/politics/2019/09/new-yorks-efforts-to-snuff-out-smoking/176923/.

4. Lauren Thomas, "Danny Meyer's Union Square Hospitality Group to Require Boosters for Workers, Diners," CNBC, December 22, 2021, https://www.cnbc.com/2021/12/22/danny-meyers-ushg-to-require-boosters-for-workers-diners.html.

5. USA Today Staff, "Read the Full Transcript from the First Presidential Debate between Joe Biden and Donald Trump," *USA Today*, September 30, 2020, https://www.usatoday.com/story/news/politics/elections/2020/09/03/presidential-debate-read-full-transcript-first-debate/3587462001/.

Chapter 3

1. Melissa Dahl, "Elizabeth Gilbert on the Link between Creativity and Curiosity," The Cut, September 23, 2015, https://www.thecut.com/2015/09/how-curiosity-leads-to-creativity.html.

2. Cordele Glass, "Creativity and the Natural Outdoors," *Positive Psychology News*, January 24, 2020, https://positivepsychologynews.com/news/cordele-glass/2020012440097.

3. Alison Pearce Stevens, "Learning Rewires the Brain," *Science News Explores*, September 2, 2014, https://www.sciencenewsforstudents.org/article/learning-rewires-brain.

4. Alexandra Akinchina, "Reading Enhances Imagination," World Literacy Foundation, April 8, 2021, https://worldliteracyfoundation.org/reading-enhances-imagination/.

Chapter 4

1. Jennifer Liu, "These Are the 12 Companies Workers Don't Want to Leave," CNBC, February 20, 2020, https://www.cnbc.com/2020/02/20/these-are-the-12-companies-workers-dont-want-to-leave.html.

2. "Cancel Culture," Dictionary.com, July 31, 2020, https://www.dictionary.com/e/pop-culture/cancel-culture/.

3. Ken Mondschein, "Getting Cancelled in the Middle Ages," Medievalists.net, n.d., https://www.medievalists.net/2021/02/cancelled-middle-ages/.

4. Arianna Huffington, "A Culture without the Possibility of Redemption Is a Toxic Culture," Thrive, August 31, 2021, https://thriveglobal.com/stories/arianna-huffington -cancel-culture-redemption-forgiveness-growth/.

5. "Statement from Dr. Seuss Enterprises," March 2021, https://www.seussville.com /statement-from-dr-seuss-enterprises/.

6. Ben Peterson, "How to Build Productivity through Rewards and Recognition," Inc., April 14, 2017, https://www.inc.com/ben-peterson/how-to-build-productivity-through -rewards-and-recognition.html.

7. Jodi Glickman, "Be Generous at Work," hbr.org, June 8, 2011, https://hbr.org/2011/06 /be-generous-at-work.

8. Albert Bourla, "The CEO of Pfizer on Developing a Vaccine in Record Time," Harvard Business Review, May–June 2021, https://hbr.org/2021/05/the-ceo-of-pfizer-on -developing-a-vaccine-in-record-time.

Chapter 5

1. Kate Kelly and Shelly Branch, "Agony of the Feet: Fashion Says If the Shoe Fits, What's the Point," Wall Street Journal, August 8, 2003, https://www.wsj.com/articles /SB106028946810231700.

2. Kelly and Branch, "Agony of the Feet."

3. Mayo Clinic Staff, "Meditation: A Simple, Fast Way to Reduce Stress," Mayo Clinic, April 29, 2022, https://www.mayoclinic.org/tests-procedures/meditation/in-depth /meditation/art-20045858.

4. Adam M. Mastroianni et al., "Do Conversations End When People Want Them To?," PNAS 118, no. 10 (March 1, 2021), https://www.pnas.org/content/118/10/e2011809118.

5. Kara Swisher, "Full D8 Interview Video: Facebook CEO Mark Zuckerberg," All Things Digital, June 10, 2010, https://allthingsd.com/20100610/full-d8-video -facebook-ceo-mark-zuckerberg/.

6. Kevin Rose, Cecilia Kang, and Sheera Frenkel, "Zuckerberg Gets a Crash Course in Charm. Will Congress Care?," New York Times, April 8, 2018, https://www.nytimes .com/2018/04/08/technology/zuckerberg-gets-a-crash-course-in-charm-will-congress -care.html.

7. Brian Tayan, "The Wells Fargo Cross-Selling Scandal, Harvard Law School Forum on Corporate Governance," February 6, 2019, https://corpgov.law.harvard.edu/2019/02/06 /the-wells-fargo-cross-selling-scandal-2/.

8. Reuters Staff, "BP CEO Apologizes for 'Thoughtless' Oil Spill Comment," Reuters, June 2, 2010, https://www.reuters.com/article/us-oil-spill-bp-apology/bp-ceo-apologizes -for-thoughtless-oil-spill-comment-idUSTRE6515NQ20100602.

9. "Andrew Cuomo Apologises over Harassment Allegations but Refuses to Resign," Guardian, March 3, 2021, https://www.theguardian.com/us-news/video/2021/mar/03 /andrew-cuomo-sexual-harassment-allegations-apology-resign-video.

Chapter 6

1. Abhimanyu Ghoshal, "Airbnb Is Taking Down Its Condescending Ads in San Francisco," TNW, October 22, 2015, https://thenextweb.com/news/airbnb-is-taking-down -its-condescending-ads-in-san-francisco.

2. Steph Cockroft, "Tesco under Fire after Selling Smokey Bacon Flavour Pringles as Part of a Special Ramadan Promotion," Daily Mail, June 24, 2015, https://www.dailymail .co.uk/news/article-3137718/Tesco-underfire-selling-smokey-bacon-flavour-Pringles -special-Ramadan-promotion.html.

Chapter 7

1. Pratik Kothari, Stephen P. Ferris, and Don M. Chance, "Bragging Right: Does Corporate Boasting Imply Value Creation?," *Journal of Corporate Finance* 67 (2021): 101863, https://www.researchgate.net/publication/348568316_Bragging_rights_Does_corporate _boasting_imply_value_creation.

2. Robert Langreth and Riley Griffin, "Pfizer Won the First Round, but Moderna Sees Final Victory Ahead," *Bloomberg*, October 29, 2021, https://www.bloomberg.com/news /articles/2021-10-29/pfizer-won-the-first-round-but-moderna-sees-final-victory-ahead.

3. Langreth and Griffin, "Pfizer Won the First Round, but Moderna Sees Final Victory Ahead."

4. Warren Buffett, "The Giving Pledge," https://givingpledge.org/pledgers.

5. Marguerite Ward, "5 Communication Tricks Warren Buffett and Other Successful Leaders Use to Get Ahead," CNBC, May 1, 2017, https://www.cnbc.com/2017/05/01/5 -communication-tricks-warren-buffett-used-to-get-ahead.html.

6. Karen Berman and Joe Knight, "Financial Communication, Warren Buffett Style," hbr.org, March 4, 2010, https://hbr.org/2010/03/financial-communication-warren.

7. Tom Kludt, "Brian Williams Controversy: Here's What We Know," CNN Business, February 9, 2015, https://money.cnn.com/2015/02/09/media/brian-williams-scandal/index .html.

8. Tia Ghose, "Braggers Gonna Brag, but It Usually Backfires," *Live Science*, May 15, 2015, https://www.livescience.com/50848-bragging-annoys-people.html.

Chapter 8

1. Jennifer Aaker and Naomi Bagdonas, *Seriously: Why Humor Is a Secret Weapon in Business and Life* (New York: Penguin Random House, 2021), viii.

2. Erma Bombeck Collection, https://ermabombeckcollection.com/life/career/.

3. Erma Bombeck Writing Competition, https://www.wclibrary.info/erma/; Erma Bombeck Writers' Workshop, University of Dayton, https://udayton.edu/artssciences /initiatives/erma/.

4. Betty-Ann Heggie, "The Benefits of Laughing in the Office," hbr.org, November 16, 2018, https://hbr.org/2018/11/the-benefits-of-laughing-in-the-office.

5. Paul Harris, "Barack Obama Accused of 'Renting Out' Ambassador Roles," *The Observer*, November 28, 2009, https://www.theguardian.com/world/2009/nov/29/barack -obama-ambassadors-role-accusation.

6. Dana Perino, *And the Good News Is . . . : Lessons and Advice from the Bright Side* (Southern Pines, NC: Twelve, 2015).

Chapter 9

1. I need to roll some credits here and thank Alan Fleischmann and Ryan Velasco from the Laurel Strategies Group for their help in conceiving and facilitating the film, and Tom Yellin and Jesse Sweet from The Documentary Group for their skillful storytelling.

2. Jill Colvin, "Bad Messaging and 'Bloomberg Fatigue': The Decline of Christine Quinn," *Observer*, September 11, 2013, https://observer.com/2013/09/bad-messaging-and-bloomberg -fatigue-the-decline-of-christine-quinn/.

3. Alex Ronan, "The Art of the Obituary: An Interview with Margalit Fox," *Paris Review*, September 23, 2014, https://www.theparisreview.org/blog/2014/09/23/the-art-of-the -obituary-an-interview-with-margalit-fox/.

4. Bob Morris, "How the Celebrity Funeral Became the New Royal Wedding," *Town & Country*, August 16, 2017, https://www.townandcountrymag.com/society/money-and-power /a10364103/celebrity-rich-people-funerals/.

5. Neil Koenig, "Next Silicon Valleys: How Did California Get It So Right?," BBC, February 9, 2014, https://www.bbc.com/news/technology-26041341.

Chapter 10

1. Alison Durkee, "Here Are the Biggest Groups That Are Still Refusing the Covid-19 Vaccine, Poll Finds," *Forbes*, June 11, 2021, https://www.forbes.com/sites/alisondurkee /2021/06/11/here-are-the-biggest-groups-that-are-still-refusing-the-covid-19-vaccine-poll -finds/?sh=36e1f05342cc.

2. "Pressure on Good Science during a Pandemic Is Leading to Confusing, and Conflicting Advice on Covid-19," *Time*, June 11, 2020, https://time.com/5851849 /coronavirus-science-advice/.

3. Zoe Strozewski, "WHO Warns against Widespread Use of Booster Shots to Avoid Vax Shortage in Poorer Nations," *Newsweek*, December 9, 2021, https://www.newsweek.com /who-warns-against-widespread-use-booster-shots-avoid-vax-shortage-poorer-nations -1657858.

4. Jamey Keaton, "Vaccine Alliance Chief: Omicron Could Trigger 'Inequity 2.0,'" AP News, December 15, 2021, https://apnews.com/article/coronavirus-pandemic-business -health-pandemics-7640f940192fc5e787d03fc402773691.

5. USA Today Network Ventures Staff, "Alabama's Dorothy Oliver Named Best of Womankind, Gets Special Nod from Dr. Fauci, during USA Today's Best of Humankind Awards," *USA Today*, December 9, 2021, https://www.usatoday.com/story/life/humankind /2021/12/09/alabamas-dorothy-oliver-wins-best-humankind-award-vaccination-effort /8889803002/.

INDEX

Aaker, Jennifer, 133
Abdul-Jabbar, Kareem, 184
abecedarians, 54–55
Abzug, Bella, 140
accents, 107
ACT UP, 23
advertising
    Covid-19 PSAs, 121–122, 183
    humor in, 139–140
    talking down to people in, 104
Advertising Age, 32
Advertising Council, 125
agendas
    resisting others', 70
    sharing, 70
AIDS, 7, 22, 23
AIDS Coalition to Unleash Power. *See* Act Up
Albright, Madeleine, 130
American Express, xvi, 88–89, 92–93, 156
    pitch at, 98–101
    360-degree feedback at, 36–37
American Federation of Teachers, 8–9
And the Good News Is . . . (Perino), 108–109
Angelou, Maya, 65
anti-Semitism, 143–144
apartheid, 7
apologies, 91, 126–127
appreciation, showing, 61–62
attitude, 42, 102–103
"At Wit's End" (Bombeck), 136
authenticity, 167

Bagdonas, Naomi, 133
Berkley, Seth, 178
Berkshire Hathaway, 114–115
Bernstein, Carl, 106
Biden, Joe, 15, 34–36, 64, 169–177
    Jha appointed by, 184
    on vaccine mandates, 179

Big Magic: Creative Living Beyond Fear
    (Gilbert), 42
Bill & Melinda Gates Foundation, 130
BioNTech, 121
blaming, 66–69, 70
Bloomberg, Michael, 14–15, 155, 164
blurting, 79
boasting, 112, 117–119
Bombeck, Erma, 135–136
Bourla, Albert, 153
    accent of, 107
    Biden's visit and, 172, 174, 175
    as CEO of the Year, 185
    documentary interview of, 151–152
    Five-Point Collaboration Plan
        and, 113
    humor and, 132–133
    Jha and, 183–184
    letter to Pfizer employees by, 35–36
    parents' story, 166
    positive attitude of, 103
    purpose statement of, 10–11
    on taking credit, 70–71
    Trump's statements on vaccines
        and, 34–36
    vaccine pledge by, 3–4
    on values, 145–146
    war in Ukraine and, x
Bradley, Kay, 159
braggarts, 117–119
Branch, McKinley, 159–160
Branch, Shelly, 73–76
brands, communicating about, 167
British Petroleum (BP), 87–88, 90–92
Brooklyn Nets, 124–125
Brown, Josh, 179–182
Brown, Ron, 90
Buffett, Warren, 114–115
Bush, Barbara, 127

Business Roundtable, 85
Buttigieg, Pete, 15, 23–24

cadence, 106–107
callout culture, 66–69
cancel culture, 66–69
candor, 19–38
    corporate, 31–36
    corporate speak vs., 33–34
    Jong-Fast and, 25–27
    last chances and, 37–38
    Meyer and, 27–29
    receiving feedback and, 36–37
    taboo topics and, 29–31
    value of, 22–25
Capehart, Jonathan, 82, 158–161
Carter, Jimmy, 115–116
The Carter Center, 116
Catmull, Ed, 133
Charles Pfizer & Company, 150–151
Chenault, Ken, xvii, 98–101, 157
Churchill, Winston, 151
"Citizenship in a Republic" (Roosevelt), 185
civility, xi–xii, 169–177. See also manners
    disagreement and, 179–185
    manners and, 57–72
Civil Rights Act of 1964, 108
clarity, 16–17, 70
    corporate speak vs., 33–34
clinical trial volunteers, 25–27
Clinton, Bill, 87
Clinton, Hillary, 95–98, 126–127
CNN, 91–92
coming out, 19–25
command centers, 89–90
communication
    civility and, xi–xii
    clarity in, 16–17, 33–34, 70
    courage and, 19–38
    about Covid-19, xviii
    curiosity and creativity in, 39–56
    with empathy and respect, 120–121
    humility in, 129–130
    intention in, 1–17
    leadership and, x–xi, xvi–xviii
    listening in, 31
    manners and, 57–72
    pitch in, 95–109
    rebuilding trust and, 3–8
    silence in, 78–79
    with stakeholders, 7–8
    on taboo topics, 29–31

techniques for, xvi–xvii
transparency in, 9–10
what not to say and, 71
community, 65–66, 137–138, 166–167
The Company I Keep: My Life in Beauty
    (Lauder), 58–59
condescension, 103–104
Connect First: 52 Simple Ways to Ignite
    Success, Meaning, and Joy at Work
    (Katzman), 102
connections, 10, 65–66, 102
    humor and, 135–137
context, 104–105
    humor and, 131–133
The Conversation: How Seeking and Speaking
    the Truth about Racism Can Radically
    Transform Individuals and Organizations
    (Livingston), 30–31
conversational language, 107–108
corporate affairs groups, 7
corporate culture, 105–106, 168
corporate speak, 33–34
courage, 19–38
    candor and, 25–27
    coming out and, 19–25
    last chances and, 37–38
    Meyer and, 27–29
    taboo topics and, 29–31
Covid-19 pandemic, xiv–xv, 185–187
    Biden's visit to Pfizer and, 169–177
    clinical trial volunteers in, 25–27
    comedy club in, 137–138
    creating advocates and, 7–8
    declaration of, 2
    documentary on, 149–154
    early weeks of, 1–4
    Five-Point Collaboration Plan and,
        112–114
    launching the breakthrough initiative
        during, 8–13
    mental health and, 183
    Meyer on, 28–29
    proof of vaccination and, 28–29
    public service campaign, 121–122
    reflective conversations on, 161–163
    remote working during, xv–xvi
    sharing the limelight in, 123–124
    Trump's statements on vaccines and, 34–36
    vaccine development, 3–13, 112–114,
        149–154
    vaccine skepticism and, 177–185
    vaccine use authorization, 63–64

cow story, 131–133
The Creative Habit (Tharp), 46–47
creativity, 39–56
    cultivating, 54–56
    inquiry and, 51–54
    learning, 44–45
    rituals for, 45–46
    senior interns and, 47–51
credibility, 161
crises
    checklist for, 86–93
    command centers for, 89–90
    pitch, in response to, 98–101
    response assessment, 92–93
    response frameworks for, 83–86
    training for, 92–93
    victim focus in, 90–91
Critchlow, Paul, 47–51
Cuban, Mark, 70
cultural considerations, 104–105, 144
Cuomo, Andrew, 91
curiosity, 39–56, 187
    of Biden, 175
    creativity and, 44–47
    cultivating, 54–56
    going to the source of, 42–44
    inquiry and, 51–54
    senior interns and, 47–51
    travel and, 39–42, 43–44

Dallas Mavericks, 70
Data and Safety Monitoring Board (DSMB),
    152–153
DDB Worldwide, 139
de Blasio, Bill, 28, 155
Deepwater Horizon oil spill, 87–88, 90–92
defensiveness, 69
DeGeneres, Ellen, 23
Desmond-Hellman, Sue, 130
details
    alienating, 71
    seeking, 55–56
    in thank-you notes, 62
The Devil Wears Prada (movie), 134–135
Dicks Street Show, 137–138
dinnertime rituals, 42–43
diplomatic appointments, 141–143
Disney Corporation, 86–87, 105
The Documentary Group, 151–154
Dolsten, Mikael, xvii–xviii, 11, 153
Donnelly, Liza, 141
Don Quixote (Cervantes), 186

drafts, reviewing, 128–129
"Drawing on Humor for Change"
    (Donnelly), 141
Dunn, Anita, 81–82, 102

Eagleton, Thomas, xii–xiii, 22
Economist, 163–164
Effron, Cheryl, 13
Eisenhower, Dwight D., 86
Ek, Daniel, 86
The 11th Hour with Brian Williams, 117
Emanuel, Rahm, 91–92
empathy, 120–121
ending on a high note, 108–109
Ephron, Nora, 106–107
Erhart, Charles, 150–151
Estée Lauder Companies, xiii–xiv, 39–42
    Roth on, 52–54
    thank-you notes at, 57–63
    Wall Street Journal story and, 73–76
Everything Is Copy documentary, 107

Facebook, 105–106
fact gathering, 88–89
Fast Company, 50–51
Fauci, Anthony, 184
feedback, 36–37
    accepting, 129
    finding truth-tellers for, 125–130
filibusters, 108
Floyd, George, 29–30
forgiveness, 66–69
Fox, Margalit, 164
frameworks, crisis preparation and,
    83–86
Francis, Pope, 183
Franklin, Benjamin, 80
Freeman, Cliff, 139
French Culinary Institute, 54–55

Garrison Institute, 78
Gavi, 178
Gay Pride movement, 23
Geisel, Theodor (Dr. Seuss), 67
Gelwicks, Andrew, 24–25
Ghebreyesus, Tedros Adhanom,
    178
Gibbs, Robert, 142–143
Gilbert, Elizabeth, 42, 107
Girls Who Code, 130
Goodall, Jane, 116
good news, leading with, 71

graciousness, 69–72, 102–103. *See also*
    manners
Grant, Adam, 106, 170–171
*The Grass Is Always Greener Over the Septic
    Tank* (Bombeck), 135
gratitude, 57–63, 187
    at Pfizer, 62
    at work, 61–62, 70–71
Gruber, Bill, 12, 153
gun violence, 7–8

Habitat for Humanity, 116
Hager, Jenna Bush, 184
happiness, 62
harmony, 169–177. *See also* manners
    disagreement and, 179–185
    as a goal, 170–171
    humor and workplace, 134–140
Harvard Business Review, 70–71
Hathaway, Anne, 47
Hawthorne, Nathaniel, 66
Hayward, Tony, 88, 90–92
help, asking for, 81–82
herd immunity, 178–179
*Hers to Lose: A Look at Christine Quinn's
    Failed Campaign for Mayor* (documen-
    tary), 154–156
history, reflecting on, 165–168
Hobson, Mellody, 130
Hoge, Stephen, 113
Hollings, Fritz, 143–144
hope, 103
Huffington, Arianna, 67
Huffington Post, 126
humility, 64, 111–130, 181, 187
    braggarts and, 117–119
    of Buffett, 114–115
    of Carter, 115–116
    feedback and, 125–130
    of Goodall, 116
    hearing other perspectives and,
        120–122
    humor and, 138–139
    learning, 122–130
    at Pfizer, 112–114
humor, 105, 131–147, 181–182, 187
    context and, 131–133
    joy and, 145–147
    minefields around, 141–145
    positive effects of, 140
    for workplace harmony,
        134–140

*Humor, Seriously: Why Humor Is a Secret
    Weapon in Business and Life* (Aaker &
    Bagdonas), 133

"I Am Not a Brave Person. I Am Also Patient
    1133" (Jong-Fast), 25–26
inquiry, 51–54
inquisitiveness, 51–54
insecurity, 119, 184–185
intention and intentionality, 1–17, 181
    in bridge building, 187
    in communication, 5–8
    Covid-19 vaccine development and, 3–13
    desire for, 6
    focusing on, 17
    highs and lows of, 13–17
    holding on to, 15–16
    launching breakthrough, 8–13
    recognizing, 13–14
    skills and, 7
The Intern (movie), 47, 48
Irving, Kyrie, 124–125
isolation, 135–137, 183

Jacobellis v. Ohio, 101
Jane Goodall Institute, 116
jargon, 71
Jha, Ashish, 183–184
Johns Hopkins Medicine, 45
Johnson, Susan, 142
Jong-Fast, Molly, 25–27
journalists
    being prepared to talk to, 73–76
    thinking like, 52–54
    use of silence by, 78–79
joy, 145–147

Kallman, Kyle, 137–138
Katzman, Melanie, 101–102
Kelly, Kate, 73–76
King, Billie Jean, 162
King, Martin Luther, Jr., 44
King Lear (Shakespeare), 145
Koch, Ed, 21

language. *See also* clarity; pitch
    filler, 80
    gracious, 65–66
    jargon, 71
    lazy, 41
    pitch and, 95–109
Lankler, Doug, 153

last chances, 37–38
Lauder, Estée, xiii, 164
Lauder, Leonard, 57–61, 76, 106
leadership
    communication and, x–xi, xvi–xviii
    company character and, 10
    humility and, 117–119
    intention in, 1–17
legacy, 157–158, 166–167
Lewinsky, Monica, 87
LGBTQ+ people
    AIDS activism by, 7, 23
    coming out and, 19–25
Lifelines: A Doctor's Journey in the Fight for
    Public Health (Wen), 182
LinkedIn, 53–54, 106, 129–130, 170
listening, 41
    active, 31
    graciousness and, 66, 72
    to other perspectives, 120–122
Little House on the Prairie (Wilder), 56, 67
Livingston, Robert, 30–31
Lyle, Yolanda, 153, 172

manners, 57–72
    cancel culture and, 66–69
    graciousness and, 65–66, 102–103
    practices for communicators, 69–72
    thank-you notes and, 57–63
masks, 184, 186–187
Mastroianni, Adam M., 79
Matrix Award, 16–17
McDermott, Mike, 172
media
    being prepared for, 73–77
    in crises, 92
    embedding film crews and, 151–156
    reporters' use of silence and, 78–79
mental health, 32, 183
mentors and mentoring, 39–41
    during the Covid-19 pandemic, xv–xvi
    senior interns and, 47–51
Meta, 105–106
#MeToo, 129–130
metrics, 167–168
Metzenbaum, Howard, 143–144
Meyer, Danny, xvii, 27–29, 65–66
Meyer, Tommy, 27
Milk, Harvey, 23
mission
    communicating clearly, 69
    humility and, 114

intentionality and, 13–14
leadership driven by, 166
stakeholders and, 7–8
Mission Possible: The Race for a Vaccine (doc-
    umentary), 151–154
mistakes, 77, 124–125, 138–139
Moderna, 113–114
Money.CNN.com, 117
Mossberg, Walt, 81
movement, creativity and, 45
mRNA vaccines, 183
multitasking, 16
Murphy, Phil, 142, 143

National Basketball Association, 122,
    124–125, 184
National Black Nurses Association, 121
National Civil Rights Museum, 43–44
National Coming Out Day, 23
National Geographic (NatGeo), 149–154
National Rifle Association, 7–8
The New Abnormal podcast, 26
New York Committee in the Public Interest,
    139–140
New York Times, 25–26, 154–156, 163–164
New York Women in Communications,
    16–17

Obama, Barack, xiii, 23, 91, 126, 141–143
Obama, Michelle, 102–103, 126
obituaries, 163–165
office parties, 145
Oliver, Dorothy, 184
Oliver, Mary, 17, 51
O'Malley, Jen, 174–175
omissions, 71
O'Neill, Mike, 88–89, 92–93, 99, 100
optimism, 103
Osaka, Naomi, 32
overpreparation, 82
"oxygen mask rule," 92

pacing, 106
Parks, Rosa, 44
patronizing, 103–104
pauses, 73–93, 181, 187
    answering questions and, 80–82
    believing in, 77–80
    crisis checklists and, 86–93
    high heel story and, 73–76
    response frameworks and, 83–86
    rushing vs., 73–74

Perdue, Frank, 32
performance, boasting about, 112
Perino, Dana, xvii, 108–109, 144
perspectives. *See also* civility
    disagreement and, 179–185
    humor and, 141
    listening to other, 120–122
Pfizer, 105
    Biden's visit to, 169–177
    communicating about successes at,
        167–168
    Covid-19 and, xiv–xv, xvii–xviii
    Covid-19 vaccine development, 3–13
    cow story at, 131–133
    documentary on, 149–154
    Five-Point Collaboration Plan at, 112–114
    gratitude at, 62
    public service campaign by, 121–122
    purpose statement of, 10–11
    racism conversations at, 30
    rebuilding trust in, 3–8
    reflective conversations at, 161–163
    reputation of, 185
    response framework at, 83–86
    senior interns at, 47–51
    sharing the limelight at, 123–124
    travel for, 43–44
    Trump's statements on vaccines and, 34–36
    vaccine resistance and, 177–185
    vaccine testing at, 152–153
    values at, 85, 145–147
    war in Ukraine and, ix–xi
Pfizer, Charles, 150–151
Pfizer Foundation, 44
pitch, 95–109, 181
    Chenault and, 98–101
    components of, 101–109
Pixar Animation Studios, 133
podcasts, 12–13
    Capehart's, 158
    Jong-Fast, 26
    The New Abnormal, 26
    owning mistakes in, 124–125
    Rogan's, 86
    Think Fast, Talk Smart, 133
political patronage, 141–143
positivity, 102–103
Potato Head, Mr., 67
"The Power of Failure" (Critchlow), 50
preparation, 171–172, 181, 187
    finding a framework for, 83–86
    for questions, 80–82

Promise Me, Dad (Biden), 174
Psaki, Jen, 80, 174–175
purpose, 84
Putin, Vladmir, ix–xi

*The Queer Advantage: Conversations with
    LGBTQ+ Leaders on the Power of Iden-
    tity* (Gelwicks), 24–25
questions and questioning, 51–54
    in crisis management, 88–89
    not knowing the answers to, 80
    preparing for, 80–82
    in response frameworks, 84–85
Quinn, Christine, 154–156

racism
    courage to talk about, 29–31, 85
    humor and, 144
reality, suspending, 45–46
recognition, 61–62, 69, 70–71. *See also*
    humility
    sharing the limelight and, 123–124
reflection, 62, 149–168, 187
    documenting your history and, 151–157
    obituaries and, 163–165
    in storytelling, 150
    with teams, 161–163
    tributes and, 158–161
    on values and successes, 165–168
Reinhard, Keith, 139
*Remembrance and Renewal: American
    Express after 9/11*, 157
remote work, xv–xvi
reputation, x–xix
    Big Pharma, 3–8
    crisis response and, 86–88
resiliency, 166
respect, 120–121
response frameworks, 83–86
rituals
    for creativity, 45–46
    dinnertime, 42–43
Ritz-Carlton, 105
Rivkin, Charles, 142, 143
Rogan, Joe, 86
Rogers, Fred, 71–72
Romeo and Juliet (Shakespeare), 77–78
Romney, Ann, 126
Romney, Mitt, 126
Roosevelt, Theodore, 185
Roots and Shoots, 116
Rose, Amy, 113–114

Rosen, Hilary, 125–127
Roth, Dan, 52–54
Ru, Nathaniel, 32
Rubin, Jamie, 13
rushing, 73–93
Russell, Richard, 108

sarcasm, 143–144
Saujani, Reshma, 130
The Scarlet Letter (Hawthorne), 66
SciencePossible, 122
"Science Will Win" ad, 123–124, 177
scratching, 46–47
self-aggrandizement, 117–119
September 11 attacks, 98–101, 157
Seuss, Dr., 67
Shakespeare, William, 77–78, 145
shame, 138–139
Shaw, George Bernard, 104
Sherman, Lisa, 125, 127
silence, 78–79
    the price of, 85
silver linings, 108–109
sincerity, 119
SKDKnickerbocker, 81–82, 125
Slacik, Claudia, 54–55
smiling, 101–102
social change, 30–31, 68–69
social media, 119, 125
solutions, cocreating, 31
Spero, Joan, xvi
Spotify, 86
Springsteen, Bruce, 14, 155
Squawk Box, 28
stakeholders
    clarity with, 33–34
    communicating with, 7–8
    letters to, 34–36
    maps of, crisis response and, 90
    mission-driven, 7–8
    response frameworks and, 84
    transparency with, 9–10
Stanford Business School, 133
Steinbeck, John, 42
St. Louis Post-Dispatch, 135
"A Subdivision Algorithm for Computer Display of Curved Surfaces" (Catmull), 133
suburbs, humor about, 135–136
successes, reflecting on, 165–168
"The Summer's Day" (Oliver), 51
The Sunday Show, 159
Supreme Court, 21, 23, 101, 179

Susman, Billy, xiii
Susman, Louis, 79, 142, 143
Susman, Marjorie, 57–58
Sweetgreen, 32
Swisher, Kara, 81

Taco Bell, 105
talking down to people, 103–104
TED Talks, 141
thank-you notes, 57–63
Tharp, Twyla, 46–47
Think Fast, Talk Smart podcast, 133
time
    reserving for creativity, 46
    rushing vs., 73–93
Time magazine, 163
Today Show, 11, 159–160
tone. *See* pitch
transparency, 6
    courage and, 19–38
    with stakeholders, 9–10
travel, 39–42, 43–44, 172–173
Truman, Harry, 115
Trump, Donald, 15, 34–36, 83, 97
trust
    legacy messages and, 167
    rebuilding in Big Pharma, 3–8
truth-tellers, finding, 125–130
Tusk, Bradley, 13

Ukraine, Russian war against, ix–xi
Union Square Cafe, 27, 28, 65–66
Union Square Hospitality, 29
US Senate Banking Committee, 87

vaccines
    advocates for Covid-19, 179–185
    Biden's visit to manufacturing plant for, 169–177
    Bourla's pledge on, 3–4
    documentary on Pfizer, 149–154
    effectiveness of, 152–153
    expressing gratitude for, 63–64
    Five-Point Collaboration Plan and, 112–114
    hoarding of, 178
    mandates on, 178–179, 186–187
    Moderna, 113–114
    NBA and, 124–125
    personal attacks and, 179–185
    Pfizer's development of Covid-19, 3–13
    proof of vaccination and, 28–29

vaccines (*continued*)
   public service campaign on, 121–122
   responses to, 177–185
   sharing the limelight in, 123–124
   skepticism about, 120–122
   Trump on, 34–36
value creation, 112
values, 85, 145–147
   reflecting on, 165–168
Van Gundy, Jeff, 124–125
visuals, crisis management and, 91–92
vocabulary, 105–106
voice, 106–107
vulnerability, 31, 160–161. *See also* courage

Wagner, Jeanette Sarkisian, 39–41
Wall Street Journal, 32, 73–76, 139
Walt Disney Company, 133, 149–154
Warren, Elizabeth, 1
Washington Monthly, 116

Washington Post Live, 28
Weil, Ella, 137–138
Weingarten, Randi, 8–9
Wells Fargo, 87
Wen, Leana, 182
white supremacy, 85
"Why a 70-Year-Old Retiree Went Back to
      Work . . . as an Intern" (Critchlow),
      50–51
Wilder, Laura Ingalls, 56, 67
Williams, Brian, 117–118, 119
Williams, Serena, 14
word choice, 41, 65–66, 105–106
workplace harmony, 134–140
World Health Organization, 2, 112, 178
writing, reviewing drafts of, 128–129

#YouDo, 129–130

Zuckerberg, Mark, 81

ACKNOWLEDGMENTS

With thanks to my professional coach Melanie Katzman for her generosity in introducing me to Jill Grinberg, my extraordinary agent. Meeting Jill set my writing wheels in motion. She and her team helped me shape my proposal and deftly guided me through the publishing maze. Thanks also to my thoughtful, passionate, and kind editor Jeff Kehoe and his wonderful colleagues at HBR Press. I'm fortunate to have worked with Karen Kelly, whose dedication and editorial expertise supported me throughout the writing of this book.

I want to give a shout out to the Pfizer Corporate Affairs Team for inspiring me every day with their creativity and courage in support of our work for patients. I especially appreciate the encouragement and support I received for this book from Eric Aaronson, Mario Castro Martinez, Carolin Crockett, and especially Anneka Norgren and Elise Stage.

I owe a debt to every boss I ever had. Two of my managers were exceptional teachers, Loretta Dunn and Tom Schick. I think of them often and ask myself what they would do if they were in my shoes at any given moment.

The principles in this book are brought to life through the many experts who shared their stories. I'm grateful to these interviewees for their time and candor: Jonathan Capehart, Ken Chenault, Andrew Gelwicks, Molly Jong-Fast, Leonard Lauder, Danny Meyer, Mike O'Neill, Dana Perino, Dan Roth, Claudia Slacik, and Jeanette Wagner.

I'm grateful to those Susmans named Marjorie who kept urging me forward as a writer. I'm lucky to have my father Louis Susman, my brother Billy Susman, and my extended family for their love and encouragement. Thanks to my friends who regularly cheered this project on: John Avlon, Paul Critchlow, Chris Dryer, Alan Fleischmann, Judy Gold, Tom Healy, Fred Hochberg, Margaret Hoover, Julie Lichtstein, Melissa Moss, Sara Moss, Hilary Rosen, Ted Sann, Lisa Sherman, Bradley Tusk, Dini Von Mueffling, Gail Wasserman, and Penny Zuckerwise.

With love to my Sag Harbor writing sisters: Catherine Creedon, Susan Scarf Merrell, Jessica Soffer, Lou Ann Walker, and especially Patricia McCormack for her encouragement over the years and many long walks in the woods.

ABOUT THE AUTHOR

SALLY SUSMAN is Chief Corporate Affairs Officer at Pfizer and vice chair of the Pfizer Foundation. In 2022 *Forbes* named Susman one of the World's Most Influential CMOs for Pfizer's efforts to combat vaccine misinformation. She received the prestigious Matrix Award from New York Women in Communications in 2019 and was named a LinkedIn Top Voice that same year.

Born and raised in St. Louis, Susman graduated from Connecticut College with a BA in government and studied at the London School of Economics and Political Science. She served on Capitol Hill as a legislative assistant handling trade and foreign investment issues for the Senate Commerce Committee, then as Deputy Assistant Secretary for Legislative Affairs in the Clinton administration.

Before joining Pfizer in 2007, Susman held senior roles in communications and government relations at Estée Lauder Companies and American Express.

She currently serves as cochair of the International Rescue Committee, one of the world's largest humanitarian aid organizations, and as a member of the board of UL Solutions, a global leader in applied safety science. She is also a member of the Council on Foreign Relations.

Susman and her wife divide their time between New York City and Sag Harbor, New York, She is an avid reader and burgeoning gardener. *Breaking Through* is her first book. Visit sallysusman.com to learn more.